Seeking Spirit

A Quest Through Druidry and the Four Elements

Sandra Parsons

www.capallbann.co.uk

Seeking Spirit
A Quest through Druidry
and the Four Elements

©2000 Sandra Parsons

ISBN 186163 125 1

Cover design by Paul Mason

Published by:

Capall Bann Publishing
Freshfields
Chieveley
Berks
RG20 8TF

Contents

C

D

Introduction

This book is not intended to be definitive; it is an expression of a Druid's Path told in autobiographical form and is about ideas. There are many excellent books which deal with specific subjects in detail and I have included a list of a few of those which I have found to be particularly helpful.

There are many ways of drawing the cycle of the year, and although I feel the elements are best drawn across the cross formed by the Fire Festivals, I have opted to appoint the quadrants to the cross formed by the Solar Festivals which gives a better balance of light in the form of sunrises and sunsets across the Elements.

I have tried to include mind exercises and examples of practical experiences of working with the elements but readily concede that in assigning specific thought forms or in forming an opinion, I may be in the minority of one. What I have found to be valid for me does not make it so for anyone else; there are as many Paths as there are people.

However, I sincerely hope that you might find something in these pages to serve you well on your own Journey.

SEP

My Law

a poem attributed to a Maori

The sun may be clouded, yet ever the sun
Will sweep on its course till the cycle is run.
And when into chaos the system is hurled
Again shall the Builder reshape a new world.

Your path may be clouded, uncertain your goal;
Move on - for your orbit is fixed to your soul.
And though it may lead into darkness of night
The torch of the Builder shall give it new light.

You were; you will be! Know this while you are;
Your spirit has travelled both long and afar.
It came from the source, to the source it returns -
The spark which was lighted eternally burns.

It slept in a jewel. It leapt in a wave.
It roamed in the forest. It rose from the grave.
It took on strange garbs for long aeons of years,
And now in the soul of yourself it appears.

From body to body your spirit speeds on,
It seeks a new form when the old one has gone,
And the form that it finds is the fabric you wrought
On the loom of the mind, from the fibre of thought.
As dew is drawn upwards, in rain it descends,
Your thoughts drift away and in Destiny blends.
You cannot escape them, for petty or great,
Or evil or noble; they fashion your fate.

Somewhere on some planet, sometime or somehow
Your life will reflect your thoughts of your Now.
My law is unerring, no blood can atone -
The structure you build you will live in - alone.
From cycle to cycle, through time and through space,
Your lives with your longings will ever keep pace.
And all that you ask for, and all you desire
Must come at your bidding, as flame out of fire.

Once list' to that Voice and all tumult is done -
Your life is the life of the Infinite One.
In the hurrying race you are conscious of pause
With love for the purpose, and love for the Cause.

Your are your own Devil. You are your own God.
You fashioned the paths your footsteps have trod.
And no one can save you from error or sin
Until you have hark'd to the Spirit Within.

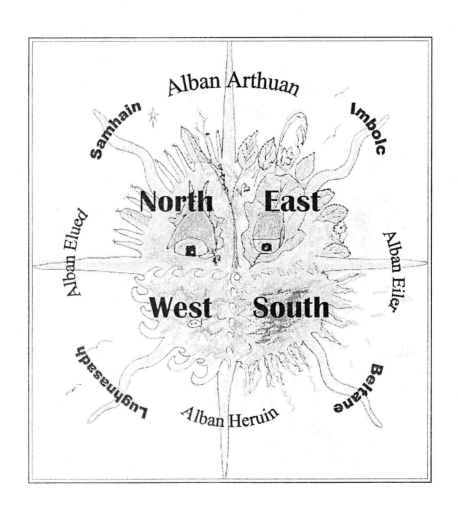

North

East

West

South

Alban Arthuan

Samhain

Imbolc

Alban Elued

Alban Eiler

Lughnasadh

Beltane

Alban Heruin

EARTH

The Cheesewring, Bodmin

NORTH - EARTH

Earth - the darkness before re-birth; the end/beginning of the cycle; the depth of darkness when the light is re-born on the shortest day. As we are born so we die to be re-born again; a perpetual cycle as seen in the depiction of yin and yang - an eternity of each containing the seed of the other - or a musical scale starting with a note, climbing through seven notes to be completed by the same one from the next octave. We start with Earth and return there, flowing through, and hopefully with, the annual cycle of seasons.

It is from the Element of Earth that we can learn of the existence of the elementals going about their business, tending and nurturing and occasionally crossing between our plane of existence and their own. It is from here we can learn of the healing properties of the plant, animal and mineral kingdoms; we can learn of the physical properties of specific plants or how their very essence can work for us on another level, and we can choose to listen to whatever these vibrations teach us.

The Earth colours are the browns, greys and black of deep earth, the muddy and muted greens and also the crisp, frosty-day colours for it is a season of sharp contrasts and not just an element with pretty little fairy creatures and splendid oak trees. There are known fears to be faced and new ones to be recognised including those regarding an awareness of our own beautiful blue and green spinning home, Earth.

An increasing number of people are developing an awareness of the planet on which we live. Even large corporate companies are recognising our need to buy products which nurture our bodies and to see this need mirrored in the preservation of our planetary home. We are increasingly aware of the inter-relatedness of all things and for some people their entry to Druidry, or other earth religion, is via this route.

Hopefully aware of the mistakes of the Past, and of the needs of suffering peoples in the Now, we are increasingly looking to the longer-term issue of sustainability and generally, the Future: we are planting seeds for the future.

Tools and Groves

Shortly before commencing the Druid Grade I visited Ireland for the first time. The ferry crossing was incredibly awful leaving me punch-drunk due to the constant buffeting as we sailed into the face of a particularly fierce gale. Only those drunk slept that night. We had already booked the first night in Blarney and having extracted the car from chaos on the ferry, assessed the damage and somehow crossed Cork City, my cousin and I went straight to the Castle's ancient Yew Grove to recover from our ordeal.

I cannot begin to express the bliss of simply sitting still. I closed my eyes to meditate for a few moments and a column of six to eight Druids immediately processed into the inner Grove of my mind from the North East, walked in single file in front of me, around behind me, and then in front of me, encircling me completely within the figure '6'. As soon as they had all completed the figure, the formality broke down and there was much laughing and chatting in the manner of a reunion. I heard my cousin come into the physical Grove where I was sat, I muttered an internal 'thank you' to those I had seen a moment before and opened my eyes. Sleep or sensory deprivation certainly enhances the connection with spirit, blasting away our usual inhibitions and ego and

8

enabling spirit to better register through our consciousness. Whereas our Ancestors may have accessed the Otherworld through darkened chambers, these days a gruelling ferry trip certainly works as well!

The whole Blarney Castle area was incredibly lovely that evening and I was filled with peace. The two wedding parties taking their final photographs eventually left and the Yew Grove seemed to overflow with rabbits. I saw my first mink and became increasingly aware of all manner of creatures living within the sanctity of the Grove. It took me several days before the experience gently released its' strong grip on my consciousness and I eased back into a more 'normal' state.

From first joining the Order of Bards, Ovates and Druids (OBOD) I felt I had 'come home', which is not uncommon for 'students of spirit', but now I felt entirely integrated within Druidry on all levels; even I, the original solitary practitioner, needed a community with which to celebrate a Rite of Passage.

As a usually solitary practitioner, partly due to my location and partly personal preference, I rarely meet with others in a physical Grove, but there is no disputing the value of meeting with people of like mind and similar interests to swap experiences and trade information. There are occasions when we all need back-up in the form of a support group or simply with people with whom we have a sense of 'belonging'. Community is something that tragically seems to be dead or dying in many areas of life. It is only when it is experienced at first hand is there realisation of what has been lost to us. A number of people have written to me to try to express their thoughts of their first Camp or Gathering. It often proves 'mind-expanding' for a first-timer as the sense of community and the level of energy raised can be beyond that previously experienced.

9

My first Pagan community weekend remains vivid in my mind for the same reasons. We finished the weekend with a closing ceremony as is usual practice so as to enable us to give thanks and also to enable us to function on a normal level sufficient to drive the car home and make the correct responses in conversation. ('Hello Officer, I'm running on pure spirit - I've been at a Pagan Camp!) Although the energy engendered during the weekend was suitably transmuted for healing or whatever, there was a part of me that stayed 'off with the fairies', a part of me touched by spirit, that actively sought spirit still more actively because of its apparent proximity that weekend.

Frequent use of a physical muscle leads to better function and for me the expansion of the 'muscle' stretching my recognition of spirit leads to better efficiency of connection. But it is more a flow of energy, a vibration, which is sought on a repeatable basis and the only restriction is our ability to recognise it. It

Roundhouse, Pembrokeshire

Roundhouse, Pembrokeshire

pays to keep the muscle working and community helps to do this by stimulating the contact.

Where possible the Druid community meets to celebrate the seasonal festivals or at other important times in the lives of the Grove members. Either meeting as a group of people in someone's house or when possible, within a grove of trees, it is a time to meet, swap ideas and generate a lot of energy. It provides a place to experience and share a Rite of Passage. The Church recognises the Rites of marriage, death and baptism but there is no reason why other Rites should not be acknowledged in community. Pregnancy, puberty, retirement and as many more occasions as are significant for an individual, can be acknowledged within a Grove and celebrated either in front of witnesses in ceremony or in some cases, quietly and apparently alone.

The Grove community is the route by which many people study Druidry and learn and experience from earth based initiation providing a good solid, 'grounding' from which to later learn to fly. The Grove, in meditation, is an equally major concept in Druidry, providing a place of security from which to journey through meditation, a haven to return to following such travels or in which to practice specific exercises.

In my meditation I have created a readily accessible meditation Grove for each Druid Grade, each distinct and separate but part of a whole picture, a little Bothy where I keep a robe and some chickens which often travel with me in meditation (no eagles or wolves for me!). There is also a large community roundhouse where the smoke from the central fire seeps through the thatch and in the comparative darkness of the place, we are safe and together. A number of us congregate here in spirit, sometimes making music, or telling tales, but usually just to be together. Who these people are I would not like to say. Perhaps they are others working within

Druidry, aspects of myself, or even a host of other incarnations from my same soul source. Whoever they are, we are community, coming and going about our business as necessary but returning to the communal hut to 're-group' our energies.

It is from the grounding of the element of Earth that we learn to invoke (bring in) and evoke (from within) a specific vibration to use for journeying shamanically. To travel as owl on silent wings in visualisation, to turn with the sun as sunflower or shamble along a forest path as bear is an enriching experience. We can locate our calm centre within, encircled by the loving arms of the Goddess and learn to fly out with the knowledge that we have somewhere safe to which to return. But in case it all seems a little too rosy, let me swiftly point out that it is not. It is the place from which to experience her in her triple form as maiden, mother and as crone.

Through working with the Element of Earth we encounter some of our greatest fears, such as our own death, learning, and in assimilating this learning, emerging stronger and empowered. These areas of our being should never be accessed at a time when we are unwilling to examine them, when it 'feels wrong', without the support of a Guide - physical or otherwise - or encountered from a base which we might intuitively consider 'unsafe'. Anything suggested, especially if a student feels unsure, or is in any way against his or her will, should be carefully examined for ultimately the experience is personal, and no one should be afraid to say 'No!' But to enable us to confront some of our deep hurts and anguish, some of the pain we encounter in life revealed by groping through the Element of Earth, we have the use of numerous tools and part of the Druid's art is to identify useful tools and those who are prepared to be our allies and work with us.

A tool is not a possession in the material sense of 'this is mine and that is yours', it is a means to an end - an axe to chop wood, a torch to light a path. It is in the reassurance it gives and the tool's function, particularly the latter, which contains the value. I have a small leather pouch which contains a few physical objects, a couple of feathers given to me by my Druid tutor for protection and shamanic flight, a beech last from a 'wishing tree' at Berry Pomeroy and various drawings of gifts given in meditation and therefore non-physical. These items are of no value whatsoever materially but shamanically they are of immense use and give me much pleasure: I consider them to be treasure trove.

I own a sword, made for me by my father, which gently dulled in the physical, is a tool of great importance with which to work shamanically. I hesitate to use the word 'weapon' for this is not the spirit of what is intended for general journeying - it is a weapon in that it is a symbol of strength, something to be wielded and an indicator of power. In journeying one does not go around randomly stabbing at things, there is the perennial question of responsibility and these tools, any of them, should be used responsibly or not at all. If one was after a weapon, common-sense would be the best one of all.

There are a great many tools available for use for body, mind or spirit. There are dozens of alternative therapies and numerous theories which can be used to promote health on a physical, emotional or spiritual level. Sometimes we come close to requiring a map to enable us to find their way through the maze of alternatives and can reach overload with all the information available. To keep new ideas flowing it becomes necessary to determine if an idea is valid in the Now and if not, to throw it into the cauldron of the mind so that as our perspective changes it can be taken out and re-examined for validity. For example a study of plants and trees often leads to some aspect of planetary, animal or human healing, involving assorted paraphernalia, a caring and compassionate nature, intent and/or a simple connection with an aspect of spirit by any one of a great number of titles. It is all as simple, or as complicated, as a student wants it to be.

For sheer simplicity, studying a tree in one's own back garden is a good place to start and with patience can lead to new insights. It is not always appropriate or even desirable to work with a tree and if having persevered there is only silence, or instinct dictates unwillingness, try another. Observe the motion of the seasons and the flow of energy within the tree and mentally reach out toward it. Sit under it, enter a meditative state and reach out lovingly. Physically hug the tree and mentally encircle it with love. (I have a very small garden with a fairly small tree. As the garden is overlooked, the whole experience necessitates crawling around looking like I'm searching for something lost - like my marbles!) Watch the blue sky or the moon and stars through the leaves and suspend logical analysis of any communication or impressions received.

It is possible to collect a number of 'friends' in this manner and it can be as exciting to visit tree friends as it is to visit human friends! Each one has their own story, their own wisdom, healing and an individual beauty of 'personality'.

Over a number of years of study a student can encounter a number of spirits of species of trees/shrubs etc. These might be experienced as a once-off meeting or there may be a more continuous alliance. Two such allies have remained with me in meditation. Gorse is a rich golden green and Reed is a splendid olive green/brown. They are an aspect of their species and although take a specific form they are more importantly, a vibrational rate producing a colour, a feeling and although I do not experience them as such, no doubt, a sound as well. I hope these allies experience a reciprocal benefit by their involvement.

Trees most often studied in Druidry are those comprising the ogham but it is possible that many of them may prove unknown to students in different countries. Where this is the case it is probably best for a student to work out their own system; nothing should be slavishly followed without querying its personal 'rightness'. The basic ogham alphabet comprises short lines and their relationship to another line. These 'letters' are drawn out and words can be built up accordingly. Although disputable as to whether or not the ogham was also a calendar in ancient times, there are various systems currently in use which do ascribe the ogham trees to particular months. My personal favourite is the Celtic Tree Oracle system by Colin and Liz Murray;. They have made their own selection of trees to months and produced a card set for divinatory use.

The species of tree experienced within a Grove meditation varies with the different Grades and need to be worked with to build and develop trust. Birch seems to be a natural favourite in the Bardic Grade. Sometimes students report their trees to be slim to start with, but in time soon swell into fine sized trees, becoming more prolific or swelling with buds which burst and become fully in leaf and magnificent - the epitome of their species. Each plant, each animal, all things experienced within the Grove are at the height of their beauty and unless specifically represented as less than perfect for a reason, they represent perfection.

When I entered the Druid Grade, the meditation Grove comprised Yew trees, and it was within the physical Yew Grove I experienced the Initiation at Blarney. It is within this Grove that Gorse and Reed come to me. This Grove is the one for magic, it is shaded and atmospheric and is the place from which I start an Otherworldly journey. Perhaps I should say that I have never physically seen a dryad, nyad, or any form of deva but through meditation at least, believe me, they are there. Within a Grove there can be a profusion of small

Ogham stone, Co. Kerry

spirits looking in or actively taking part. Sometimes people do not see animals, birds or devas but with time they are usually experienced within the Grove. Like the trees of the Grove itself, the experience swells to encompass all things. With practice, those who do not see in colour or hear natural sounds and voices do, in time, find their experience greatly enhanced.

I have 'inherited' a love of a small house-plant known as Saint Paulia, the African Violet. I have over a dozen in the house and their sheer vibrancy and eagerness makes me love them. When I decided to see if I could meet with the African Violet deva in meditation I encountered a beautiful little fairy creature, complete with wings, who was a mixture of green and a rich fuschia colour sparkling with the shining 'dust' found on many of the Violet's flower petals. She was breathtakingly beautiful and flitted around my meditation Grove in happy little bursts of energy; she was exquisite. Although I say 'she' it is not a question of being gender specific for often an essence expresses both male and female qualities and appear in a human-like form to which we can relate. The African Violet deva, while clearly female of form expressed the qualitites of both genders.

Another associated elemental energy is discovered when working with crystals. Crystal energy can be harnessed for a wide number of uses to include making essences, healing, divination and their energies can be used as wonderful amplifiers of intent. A specific thought vibration is input and the vibration is continually expressed, either into the room, or in one's pocket depending on the nature of the use. In this respect crystals are excellent for protection and healing. There are many books in print giving advice and individual properties of the use of crystals and gemstones but suffice it to say that as well as carrying a 'programmed' crystal in one's pocket or on a table in a living area, a piece of gemstone in one's pocket is vibrating at a rate of its own, and hence mixing with the wearer's vibration, may benefit the wearer by its own special properties.

Crystals can prove excellent teachers if one is responsive to the 'spirit' of the crystal. It is also possible to sit quietly with a crystal and observe them 'smoking'. No particular lighting conditions are required for this, but it is necessary to sit still for several minutes. (Crystals are affected by heat and it may be that it is the warmth of the hand holding the crystal that enhances the energy and causes it to apparently 'smoke'.)

I am fortunate to have a crystal ball which, sitting on my dining table, 'emanates' into the room. Amplifying the thought put into it, the ball seems to vibrate with love. It is also a marvellous de-stressing tool for to sit and stare into - purely to marvel at its' beauty is incredibly relaxing. The sphere would not be an especially good one for scrying for it is seriously 'stressed' with veils and planes crossing through it. It is this damage which gives it such beauty for the light passing through the planes splits and the inherent colours become visible and glow; a concept which can be highly relevant in our own experience of life!

Another treasure of immense value, and one which I hesitate to term a 'tool', is the co-operation by the wealth of animals who make themselves known in meditation as allies and lend support and an aspect of their own strength to the visualisation experience. At a very early stage I collected a sheep. Not a ram, or a lamb or indeed anything with an impressive title; a sheep. I confess to having been somewhat disappointed as, although I knew better, I still hankered after a wolf or eagle! My sheep however is magnificent; as a male sheep I suppose he is actually a ram, but remains by definition a 'sheep', with great curly horns and a wonderfully thick woolly coat. He is the epitome of 'sheep'; the biggest and brightest and best of 'sheepdom'. It took me some time to comprehend what he represented but as time passed, and we have journeyed together on many occasions, I have come to respect and care deeply for this magnificent creature. He is to 'animal' as Oak is to 'tree'. He provides a good solid partner with whom to travel offering protection and a 'no nonsense' approach. There have been occasions when I have considered myself to be a little woolly lamb to be guided by those in whom I place my trust, and I could find no better Guide than my sheep. Although my sheep was the first animal to appear to me, closely followed by a couple of chickens, there have been a number who have come and gone, who added something to my learning for a period of time and having accomplished their mission, gently withdrew again. All were completely trustworthy.

Trust is a really weird thing - it cannot be bought or sold but is in itself a tool which can be worked with. At heart it just is. A person either trusts someone or something, or doesn't. I trust my Gods to look after me, and this gives me a valuable tool to use. Some people can be trusted with money but not secrets and other people can be trusted with one's life but not with one's love; the trick is in knowing the nature of the person concerned and whether or not they have a price which could result in their being very free with one's trust.

It seems that a large percentage of people, especially women, have a problem with trust. I like to think, as do most of us, that I do not have a lot of 'baggage' - the sort of 'chip on the shoulder' sort of thing. Rubbish! One day I was speaking to someone who said 'but then, of course, you have a problem with Trust'. I was aghast, but on close examination I found it was absolutely true and that it was not only inherent in my genetic make-up but had been built upon by personal experience. A great many (and often unlikely) people have a woolly lamb inside them, innocent and trusting and often heart-wounded as a result. Somehow we should find a way to acknowledge this inside ourselves, both in recognising the childlike quality within and the need for that child to be allowed to come out to play on occasion. Trust is one of the issues faced in the Grove and which appears and reappears through the cycle of seasons in all its myriad forms.

A more physical tool amongst those available to the student Druid is the dowsing rod or pendulum. The whole concept of dowsing is pretty inexplicable and there seem to be as many answers as to why it works as there are dowsers - but work it does. Useful for finding water, map dowsing, finding out information about another person's health, ie what is wrong, what needs to be done and even doing it is all part of the dowsing experience. A sacred space created for ritual and ceremony is dowseable. A circle created by intent of the mind and a finger tracing an outside edge of a working space, can be easily recognised by dowsing rods. After the circle has been unwound the rods indicate there is nothing there.

For me dowsing provides a heightened experience of earth energies which can be felt at a site but for which I would like to see some kind of 'physical' evidence. I am certainly no professional dowser, more a progressional one. I do not use the art sufficiently to be entirely proficient but I do enjoy what I can do. If I exercised the skill more I would get better results and although a serious subject, it is fun. Following the reading of a superb book translated into English entitled 'Points of Cosmic Energy' by Blanche Merz, my mother and I became keen on dowsing a site for its vibrational rate in Angstroms ie to which plane it best resonates be it physical, etheric or spiritual. Having looked for water sources, energy lines and how these effect the human aura (increase or other change) the plane on which it vibrates is an interesting 'find'.

Whilst I am not particularly keen on the 'have a go' theory, it is something we tend to want to do so if a person is interested in trying a skill, dowsing gives relatively little cause for concern compared to say a Ouija board. However, even this relatively 'safe' discipline can lead one to do something out of enthusiasm for the task rather than a sense of personal safety. On two occasions my mother or I have experienced ill health at a site; on each occasion we failed to request entry to the site from the genius loci, being too carried away with our enthusiasm. The first was at Pawton Quoit, near Wadebridge, Cornwall. My mother was taken ill at the Quoit and the second was when we sat under the ancient trees, Gog and MaGog at the foot of Glastonbury Tor. Having had our sandwich in the shade of the trees, we got up to leave and became suddenly unwell. The hill leading up toward the road around the Tor and the parked car became almost too steep and too far for us - even though we punctuated our return with numerous rests in the hedge On both these occasions a simple 'may we enter here?' would have prevented our enthusiasm rushing us into incompatible energies.

When we first started seeking a physical indication of energy fields, in this case the human aura, we began with a 'Twizzle' stick. This is a splendid device - although close to being a dubious party trick. The Twizzle stick is as eccentric as its creator cares to make it. It comprises a length of wire attached to a stick and a crystal strapped onto the free end of wire. The idea is that the wire can have as many bends and twists in it as wanted and results in it being almost completely unstable and therefore not something that can be influenced by the hand that holds it. When the crystal on the end of the wire is slowly brought into contact with the aura of a willing volunteer it registers the outside edge and however much nearer it is persuaded to go, it pulls itself away to return to the outside edge. A great way to begin recognising energy fields but as previously said, something of a party trick.

Sometimes there is a need for a little physical drama, a theatrical gesture and a few words of seemingly appropriate terminology. This is fine assuming the content is understood for what it is and not assumed to be what it is not; a little incense goes a long way. Creating atmosphere with music and assorted paraphernalia is a time-honoured method of inducing the appropriate thoughts but there have been so many programmes on the TV on the subject of esoterica, complete with nearly blanket-thick smoke, eerie music, perhaps even the odd skull lying around in casual fashion, as to be positively toe-curling. Much of what is practised is spontaneous and natural. A little theatre evokes atmosphere and focuses the mind, like peering at tea leaves to scry, and what one does in one's own home environment is entirely one's own business, but as a general guideline, if you cannot see across the room for smoke, open a window before a neighbour calls the Fire Brigade!

We comprise many parts which can be represented by specific personality types and for some of us the performer is inherent and indeed, necessary in our ceremony. A knowledge of one's own personality types proves a useful tool both in knowing which aspect of oneself to use in a given situation or equally which not to use. Initially several personality types present themselves and over time others literally, become apparent. A considerable degree of honesty is required in such work. I have a Circle of Seven - this being the number of represent-atives on a continuous basis supplemented by others who come and go or who are represented by one of the main seven. Given a specific problem I call a meeting and attempt to distance my ego from the problem in question. Each representative sits at a Round Table and has equal say, although a given problem will affect some more than others.

My major players comprise a Princely Druid (who displays many qualities of the South and who is the arbitrator if necessary), a Hedgewitch (a practical Wise Woman), a Gardener (who cares and nurtures in a practical way and who can carve a piece of wood into something useful or reel off a list of physical qualities of different woods), a Warrior Queen (who displays fight and nerve but needs tempering at times), an 'Ivory Tower' Princess (who is interested in myth, legend and heroic deeds to the exclusion of practicality), a meticulous Secretary who sends out all the Agendas on time (and is efficient to the point of being irritating) and finally, but certainly not least in the Circle, is a little woolly lamb type, an Innocent, a trusting little soul doomed to a measure of hurt and disappointment (much as The Fool of the Tarot cards) and probably represents intuition. In many respects this is the truest (deepest) element of my own being and the one who tends to sit quietly at the Table. This little soul is cared for by the others who tend to be noisier and more bold but the little lamb does bring out the best in the loving side of the others. There is room for all parts at the meeting. All are equal but have different qualities to bring to the table.

The imagery is a useful tool but perhaps I should point out that the use of apparent 'royalty' is merely indicative of strong archetypes (which can also be seen to represent cardinal directions) rather than past-life lineage! Whatever decision is reached, when all parties who wish to speak have been heard, it will be the best guidance for the circumstances and the results are greater than the sum of the parts. It is up to me to go with them or come to my own conclusions in less clear a manner.

It is readily obvious how decisions can be made by 'listening' to several of the most applicable 'characters'. Some decisions would probably be made by the 'Royals' (Druid Prince, Warrior Queen and Ivory Tower Princess), more practical matters by the Gardener, the Secretary or the Hedgewitch, decisions regarding health by the Druid, Hedgewitch or Gardener etc. You can see how lines can be drawn linking the characters across the Table and in so doing it can be seen if one predominates and should perhaps give another more of a chance to speak. Lamb speaks seldom, very tentatively but is usually heard by everyone present - the Druid Prince is the obvious key player but when little lamb speaks, it is such an occurrence that everyone will usually go along with what is said. It can be a well-enacted drama capable of a very 'just' resolution to a problem - a mind-game with 'Air' sign written all over it.

(At the time of manifesting my Circle of Seven I had not come across the concept before and thought it to be a useful tool of my own. What conceit! There is a version within the Druid Course I later studied and I have since discovered its' wider use. There are some excellent books on the subject which detail ways of exploring different aspects of one's character at differing levels, some of which being represented by characters from a specific theme eg characters from Arthurian legend/Grail stories etc. I felt like the one hundredth monkey, washing my potato or yam in the water at the same time as others already washing theirs all across the world - an unoriginal original thought?). The idea of calling a Gathering is not for everyone - what is? For those who do find it useful, it can be of immeasurable value. As an 'Air' sign and living much of my life in my mind I am lucky (or am I?) to have a vivid imagination and I suspect such tools would appeal more to those of an 'airy' nature.

Visualisation and the creative arts are high on the Agenda in Druidry and for someone with an acutely analytical mind much of what is witnessed or heard could be dismissed as whimsical and lacking in scientific proof. For someone such as my father my mind games are not useful, they are plainly incomprehensible but he is developing other elements and although he will probably never really understand my nature, or I his, we can meet part way in our understanding of the other. Thankfully most people display aspects of all the elements in greater or lesser parts and it never fail to impress me when someone who is not so obviously inclined to right brain activity perseveres and enhances another aspect of themselves.

My father is born under the sign of Aries and is a pioneer, an inventor (he can become really excited when discussing the possibilities of methane), immensely practical, keen to take something apart to see how it works, and displays left brain tendencies on a general basis. For years we went to a meditation class and he persevered with visualisation although with only little success. Eventually he stopped but slowly ventured into creating things which he would have once considered to be 'useless' works of art. He has created a number of pieces of work which, because of his practical nature, are superbly crafted and to a very high standard. He made me a sword as I have mentioned elsewhere and given motivation I could see him making shields and armour, whittling peace pipes and carving the entire contents of a Noah's Ark!

Being a beneficiary of a number of his pieces I can see he is clearly expressing the Bardic art of awakening and integrating right brain activity with his natural left brain activity. As an Aries he is my Libran opposite - how very true! We tend toward the same goals via totally different routes finding the other's road too rocky for our own choice. (I find methane of limited interest and Dad despairs of my mind games!) Our greatest lessons are to be found in each other, rounding off each other's corners, and striving for balance.

Druidry contains a lot of paradox and contradiction; understanding one opposite to comprehend the other; getting to grips with triplicities; looking outward for spirit to find it within; going inward to fly outward; studying the element of Earth to comprehend the inherent death in re-birth and the potential for life in death. Wise words, the Laws of Nature and the tools we use enable us to till the soil of Earth. We use earth, she is our home, our Mother, and she provides the basics of life for us, but this is no single-sided coin, for through her spirit flows. Death and re-birth are opposites of the same element - so are the tools for tilling and an understanding of the vibration of spirit which is Earth. Balance between the elements, balance within the same element, in our lives, in our society is the real source of learning. We need to stop separating and distinguishing between aspects, creating 'good' and 'bad' and learn to see the whole picture; we need to place less emphasis on the material and take a look at the spirit which is Earth.

The Feel of Earth

The vibration of the element of earth can be experienced at a place where there has been little change in centuries, although this need not be the case. For example, a cave or an ancient well, somewhat over-grown, still revered by a few, evokes the 'feel' of the Element earth where it meets with the Element of water.

Madron Well in Cornwall is such a place. Although somewhat silted over, it remains basically unchanged by time and is still in use today. The area is hung with 'clouties' (ribbons of cloth etc left as 'well-wishes' for the sick - as the cloth decays, the illness also dissipates) and it exudes a strange atmosphere. Many eyes seem to be watching your progress along the path and also to accompany you on your way back out toward the roadway. The first time my parents and I visited the Well we became overwhelmed by the watching eyes. We walked along the path toward the Well in single file and the further we progressed down the tree and foliage lined path the more the strange atmosphere became apparent. As is often the way when faced by something unknown we became fearful and by the time we reached the immediate environs of the Well and spotted the clouties we unanimously agreed to a strategic withdrawal, turned and fled! Madron Well is empowered by use, its memory kept alive and it is a 'working' energy. Several years on Madron's energy was the host to a wonderful 'coincidence'.

St Nectan's Glen, another ancient and atmospheric site in Cornwall, has a 'working' Earth energy which can be readily experienced as alive and vibrant. To visit requires pilgrimage, often a muddy one, through a tree-lined valley, complete with river running through it, and a persistent impression of elementals. A waterfall cascades through a circle of rock into the Kieve (rock basin), but such a description does little justice to the uniqueness and magic of the place. The area is incredibly beautiful, timeless and due in part to its dense greenery, there is a profusion of mystery. Our first visit was in sharp contrast to the Madron experience; a few years on we were, hopefully, a few years wiser, or more likely, more accustomed to experiencing energies. The sky was clouded over but as we turned the corner and made our way across the stepping stones to view the falls, the clouds parted and the sunlight streamed through the trees. The area lit up, radiant with light and the whole valley smiled for us. The clouds re-grouped and the sunlight was gone - the moment more intense for its brevity. We were enchanted by the place and only later realised that it is for a very limited period of the day that sunlight can shine into the Kieve.

The river flows down through the Glen and rushes on to meet the sea through Rocky Valley which, although distinctly different in character of landscape, is also a place of considerable presence. Presence of what or whom is up to the visitor to decide. As the river passes by a derelict mill there are 2 labyrinths carved in a rock wall. Although one may not have the same pedigree as the other, they are ancient and a feature which can be found in such diverse places such as New Grange in Ireland, Long Meg in Cumbria or Chartres Cathedral. Why would our Ancestors have carved these time-consuming symbols into the rock face in the valley? Perhaps the answer is in the question - 'time consuming symbols'. The labyrinth was obviously a sacred symbol to our Ancestors; it had to be worth the considerable effort entailed. A cross-section of our brain takes a similar form (as does a walnut!). Are these symbols a form of map illustrating the maze through which we grope our way to the centre - whatever we might perceive that to be? Is the centre our goal; a place where we can contemplate our supposed achievements and recollect our journey? Life is for me, a journey and a basic map is provided by oracles and other connections with Spirit, and also in the practice of Druidism. Sometimes I use the map but at other times I choose to wander around a bit, or stop and look at other things, lightly criss-crossing a basic, worn, earth pathway. The path (one of many) leads me to Source, whatever it may prove to be and will only become known to me (remembered by me) through the greatest, and possibly loneliest journey of all, death. It is however no linear path - it is a spiral, a maze, a labyrinth. Each single journey of a lifetime forms one loop of the maze seen in an isolation of many single journeys, ultimately comprising one great journey; it is the past, present and future forming a single whole picture.

Science informs me that the more I use my brain the more connections are created within it - the more possibilities to connect with the next loop of the labyrinth? If it is true that our brain need not deteriorate with age, and that these 'connections' are maintained, why have we lost respect for our Elders? Are they not therefore as much a rich 'resource', to be sought and appreciated, as the young for their youth and energy? Or is it that, in our disassociation with the spirit of Earth, we are cutting ourselves off from one quadrant of society? Do we only see spirit running through those in the prime of life, or still with youth, as having spirit, thus distancing ourselves still further from the spirit of earth? Be warned you future generations, I say, for I intend to die young at an advanced age having woven a very fine web of connection with spirit; I also intend to wear a purple hat and red socks if I feel so inclined!

Druidry need not be a path, a journey, Religion or Philosophy or anything else of specific label but for me the sign of the labyrinth is an indication of our own journey over Past, Present and Future. Was it the motif used by our Ancestors too? A shared reverence of symbols is evident between our cultures as increasingly more and more people find common ground and rediscover the sacred at ancient sites, re-discovering alignments, sacred proportions and energies.

I have a particular love of Quoits (Portal Dolmen), very much of the Element of Earth, and my nearest one is the Hell Stone, just over the border in Dorset. The Hell Stone may well reflect the name of the local Sun God Helis, but it is often the case that such a site has some reference to the Devil in the name, given in the common era, and indicating the structure's pre-Christian origins. What these Quoits were originally used for is a matter for some controversy. Although they may have been used to some extent as burial chambers, if only after a previous use had declined, this does not explain a number of the mysteries attached to them and why visitors return again and again. It is my belief that they were used as a focus for meeting with the Ancestors, to remain in contact and share some of their knowledge, and to evoke spirits for initiations and journeying shamanically to answer questions or provide solutions to tribal or health problems.

Another antiquity of the Element of Earth is the typically Cornish Fougou; strange underground corridors or cellars. They may have been used for storage or more likely, as the Quoits, a shamanic-style initiation; a return to the womb of the earth through which to be re-born. There is considerable historical tradition of an initiate being holed-up and through sensory deprivation, rising phoenix-like from the experience to new understanding - or insanity. The Native Americans for example have a tradition of the Vision Quest. Suitably prepared by fasting, they go out and dig their own 'grave' and lie in it overnight covered by a blanket. Their experience is closely observed and each person becomes their own shaman, guided by Guardian Spirits and given insights into the working of the cosmos. It is a re-birthing process and not surprisingly the element of earth is symbolised by Bear who hibernates in winter and rises again each spring. Bear's den is deep within the earth like the initiate using quoit or fougou to suspend 'normal' life, and he is the Arthur of legend who will return when the time is 'right'.

The Element of Earth, is not all sobriety and death, it is about a deep belly laugh at the absolute idiocy of things generally (including oneself) and this sense of humour is almost pre-requisite as we journey through life somewhere between waving or drowning, laughing or crying. A sense of (appropriate) humour is even more a requirement in Paganism - we can encounter some very odd situations and the ability to laugh is often an excellent antidote to an otherwise awkward or painful situation. Like everyone else we can take ourselves very seriously, deeply so at heart, but we must not get too bogged down with the need for respect and responsibility and the accoutrements of our 'magic'; it is fun too.

For those who prefer to approach their art 'skyclad', apart from their wellies, I envy them their courage but cannot find sufficient in me to join them. A burst of inappropriate giggling due to self-consciousness could ruin an otherwise solemn and beautiful ceremony. A thick woollen robe over 6 sweaters, a thermal vest, 2 pairs of jogging trousers and the outfit completed by 3 pairs of socks suits me much better. In this attire I know I won't have the same irreverent urge to giggle - I can't because of the weight of clothing. I know I lose spontaneity - taking five minutes to waddle around a circle - but at least I am not the one with frostbite on a frosty February evening!

We do get ourselves in some ridiculous situations in our bid to observe our faith, converse with Ancestors or energies and feel connected with the flow of our Gods and Goddesses at historical sacred sites or other appropriate places. I have leapt enthusiastically over a stile to find my hem had caught in mid flight, leaving me suspended until the material gave way, rending my outfit from hem to waist; I have waded through mud 'enhanced' by senna-pod eating cows, sufficiently deep to have given me 'mud' garters above my wellies, and have laughed myself senseless at the Hell Stone which has provoked a singular amount of silliness - largely because of the need to negotiate the bull in the field. In my experience to date (!) it is totally amiable but it is a really large one and sprawls across the footpath, blissfully dozing except to roll his little piggy eyes.

We have followed the footpath across the fields, compass in hand, to try to find out if we would be able to see the sun rise on the summer solstice. Thick, water-filled grey rolls of impenetrable sea fog from the nearby coast blew in and by the time we arrived at the Quoit, thoroughly soaked to the knees by the long grass, we knew exactly where east was but were unable to see if it corresponded with the gap in the hills. But one of the most curious things spotted from the Quoit was what appeared to be a Druids' Fun Run. We were sat quietly at the Quoit when a great many people in long white outfits started running around the nearby Hardy's Monument. We decided that one of the Druid Orders had decreed their members should take more exercise! No, doom and death may be part of delving into the element of earth, but in finding our connection with the spirit of her, we are promised a side-splitting belly laugh - especially at our own small selves.

Going with the Flow

It can be difficult to maintain a personal balance of light when faced by the carnage of some of our ancient and immensely beautiful sites - and many pagans do actively campaign for some aspect of planetary awareness, preservation or welfare. Although many ancient monuments have been 'saved' from the plough, less conspicuous sites are still facing desecration, many gone under and lost from memory; too many places lost because they are largely forgotten. To some extent, like our dead, there is still the input of power as long as there is memory but once forgotten the power is diminished; a treasured photograph of a son lost at war can become an old and useless memento several generations on, doomed to be thrown away. Energy at a site whether remembered or otherwise remains an undisputed vibration experienced by those sensitive to its pulse - this energy just is but by being unobserved it is then not as readily apparent to many people and the memory can die. As long as those places we hold sacred, indeed our land itself, are remembered or considered in some way holy by sufficient people, they will be preserved, and, given new understanding, a revival could lead to a sensitive restoration to power.

Spinster's Rock is the only Quoit in Devon and is found on the edge of Dartmoor, near Drewsteignton. It was once part of an enormous complex but almost the entire site was butchered with, presumably, a greater regard for the space it occupied than its sanctity, grubbing up its stones and casting them into the hedge. The quoit is now the single remaining structure, having been re-erected in Victorian times. Supposing some of the other original stones were still available and of course, supposing the co-operation of the current landowner and the will of a number of workers, would it be possible to recapture some of the magnificence of the original landscaped site? Would it even be right to try?

The energies must still be there and a geophysical survey would probably be able to pick up on some exact locations for specific stones. A team of experienced dowsers might be able to identify what went where and with open-mindedness and co-operation, both teams of experts could collaborate to restore a monument to something approaching its former glory, and most importantly, with respect for the sensitivity of the project. And would new stones cut with love for the project be more suitable than concrete indicators? Personally, I think that if the land were made available etc, I would be honoured to participate in the work, and in due course to help 'sing in' the placing of the stones. A fallen and undignified pile of stones may be 'original' (presumably the energy was actually what was original and the monuments erected to enhance the energy and bring it into the lives of those people who experienced it), and I am certainly not saying we should rush out and restore everything in sight, (horror!) but there are some places that should be maintained, even restored, with dignity, and in respect to the Ancestors and Gods worshipped there. It might also teach us a thing or two.

The Stanton Drew circles are expanding their energy. Through repeated ceremony their relatively dormant energy is increasingly 'alive' and accessible. It may be that their energies are being enhanced, and also now carry the vibration of our current input, so making their vibration more accessible to more of us less attuned to energies outside our usual range of sensitivity. This can be seen to be an increasingly speeding wheel of motion and if this is correct, the purpose and input etc must be tempered with caution - quartz (an important factor in our 'living' rock and stones specially selected for sacred use often have a high quartz content) amplifies the energy put into it, whatever the intent may be. Is this part of what was feared over the 'witch hunt' years, that if energy is just energy, it can be manipulated for specific use? Are we sufficiently mature now at this dawning of the new Millennium to reawaken some of these semi-dormant energies and activate their potential? Are we capable of sensible and appropriate use - and who is to say what is 'sensible' or 'appropriate'?

The accessible Lanyon Quoit in West Penwith, is magnificent, re-erected and over-used - perhaps if left collapsed a greater sanctity of the site might have been maintained but it has enabled a great many people to experience it - and perhaps to awaken something inside them. It is a site best visited late in the evening or early in the morning when the energies are either re-grouping for the day or before they dissipate. Has this site lost something for having been re-erected? Possibly, but is it better for being upright, the capstone held aloft, or for it to have been left to rot as a tribute to what used to be?

Should a site such as a holy well, be kept free of excessive greenery - a sympathetic house-keeping? If too grown in it becomes difficult to use but at least in its inaccessibility it will remain secluded and untouched. But should the energies be allowed to be forgotten or do we continue to worship our Gods, even adulterating the site by our use with candle wax etc, whilst keeping the energies alive. They will of course always remain but my point is in their relevance to the Now. Would the Goddess rather be allowed her privacy or would she rather be part of our lives? Can we cope with her energies in a more sympathetic manner in the Now or should we let her slumber longer in the hope we might improve with keeping, or will her awakening within us cause those increasingly speed-ing wheels of motion to drag us up and on to an increasing awakening in humanity.

Paganism is often thought to be a feminine/Goddess religion. Certainly this can be true but it need not be exclusively so and indeed both aspects should be represented in some form as we seek a point of balance; the mid-point of the pendulum's swing. There should be an integration of the best of both, the pendulum neither swinging wildly nor held rigidly in any one place - including that of the mid-swing by a great weight making it rigid and inflexible - but a-quiver, dancing around that central position, actively reflecting the specific needs of a particular circumstance. A fluid beauty, twinkling through movement within the light not exclusively male or female - sometimes one, sometimes another, often neither specifically yet somehow both. The sun, often portrayed as masculine, has not always been seen to be so - the meditations given later refer to the sun as 'she'. We refer to the 'man in the moon' but the reflected light is now more usually considered to be feminine. It is certainly worth looking at the masculine energy of the moon and feminine energy of the sun and explore these inner energies for future integration into ritual or ceremony.

Feminism can be about changing the world for women so we can become like men or the 'New Age Man' become more in touch with his 'feminine' nature. Each sex should be understood and respected for what it is, neither suppressed or oppressed, nor expected to behave in the manner of the other. We are ourselves, it is our tolerance, awareness and attitude which should change. We are equal, but equally we are ourselves and not each other. As we turned further and further away from the nurturing and creativity of femininity and collectively fell into the linear, analytical and material world, the world of the man exploded at the expense of spirit; meaning was lost at the expense of the letter. More recently the patriarchal and linear establishment has taken a knock and it seems that many who are prepared to see the advantages of the feminine to supplement their own under-standing, no longer know how to behave. We seem to have a growing fear of what is 'politically incorrect' and some-times seem to lose the plot entirely. Women should not need to rush out to embrace a man's world on the man's terms. Ultimately we should all be seen on our own terms - all providing the best in our natures which in a more global picture presents a whole view not particular parts expressed in a variety of ways. Women and men have a great deal to offer - by being themselves and not conforming to a gender specific preconception. Liberation is for everyone - we are strands of the same whole picture and should not feel we need to compete with the other. To compete for a job is one thing, where the most relevant individual is appointed, but to claim supremacy of gender over the other is another. And on the basis that we may not yet be mature enough to maintain a balance of 'power', should our society be organised from a matriarchal or patriarchal viewpoint? Neither single view is wholly correct but so long as we cannot see the whole picture we select a single view at the expense of the other. We adhere to and defend an isolated view at our peril; old habits die hard and social conditioning plays a large part in our thinking - it can take several generations to pass before new ideas take hold.

I still say 'Gods' as a blanket term to mean all aspects of creativity and this probably stems, at least in part, from social conditioning. It is also awkward to mutter too many 'esses' or consistently refer to 'he/she' so ultimately go with what feels right, and a flow to which I recognise no particular direction but my own. Somewhere through the terminology there is a dance of divinity where an 'ess' becomes more relevant than a God. I believe it important that we attain, sustain and maintain the movement of the pendulum and not swing violently away from one side to another. There must be room for male and female, God and Goddess, in ceremony as appropriate, in myth and legend and at core, ourselves. This is one of the key successes of Druidry for me; a recognition of flow and I think Druidry empowered by the ability to change and add or delete to keep it up-to-date and moving.

Some Druids use the image of the Holly King struggling for supremacy with the Oak King at the two Solstices, one winning over the other for six months of the year to give an annual cycle but personally I dislike the idea of marked division even if both have equal supremacy overall. Of course we have opposites, both as valid or necessary as the other and forming a complete round, but the death of one aspect seems just too severe a distinction, and just because it is traditional does not make it personally current, so this is something I do not chose to recognise. Similarly many traditional practices would be out of place now and even if we did use ancient criteria with immaculate lineage, would not be relevant today.

Some people, usually those outside Druidry, are quick to point out that our tradition is flawed, a doubtful lineage with a dubious pedigree and extensive breaks in the chain. A few others become bogged down with the link to the past and eager to be part of such a rich tradition. Whereas I do see that some people need to be part of something which is entirely defined and something rich at that, to define it's origin is somewhat irrelevant to the 'Now'. The Druids existed; it matters not whether they were the priesthood of the Celts as my dictionary states, whether they came over with the Celts in approximately 500BCE or with a longer pedigree as Proto-Druids in our lands since approximately 2000BCE. They existed, we know something of them, they are part of our Ancestral heritage and therefore part of who we are now. Part of their knowledge lives on but as the years have passed we have need for new beliefs to be integrated with old to keep things flowing.

In no way do I wish to denigrate these incredibly educated and cultured people for I have immense regard for their talents and beliefs and choose to be called 'Druid' whilst appreciating that my knowledge is appallingly poor compared to theirs. Not being tied to a Past I am concerned with the flow of the Now, incorporating the old where appropriate or not where something else is required; this is Druidry for me. Some might say this is a watered-down tradition but for me it is a rich one. There is a tremendous amount of art and information which comes under the heading of 'Celtic'. What is 'Celtic'? Again, being something that cannot be absolutely defined I think the best answer is the one of 'feel'. If something is of the Celtic style and has the right flavour to it - great. The best definition of a Celt I have heard is that of someone who 'feels' for the land with an inexpressible longing for something not quite known. This transcends the need to be a third generation anything in particular, or native to a specific region. Druidry is not exclusive. We comprise many parts as does our nation and we all have the right to declare our heritage to be flowing through us; there are a great many people who are 'Celts' at heart whatever their creed, colour or background. It is therefore impossible to have a rigid format and we need to flow with the cycle of change as we progress through our apparent linear time.

Whether we realise it or not, it seems that most of us do respond to the changing cycles of nature and by very nature of ploughing the land, sowing seeds, tending them and harvesting the crop, the subject of fertility is not too far away. This seems to be one of those subjects about which everyone has an opinion but somehow often tends to miss the finer point: whenever an ancient site is examined or discussed, someone will suggest fertility rites. Maybe they are right or at least partially right, but it sounds as though sex was the single preoccupation of the ancient (or modern Pagan) peoples! Perhaps better expressed as 'creation' rather than 'fertility' the subject opens up and becomes more readily seen to include works of art, music and other expression of right brain use. It is a matter of personal bias, we all approach things in our own way. For example, I understand that Wicca takes the act of creation as being of major importance whereas Druidry takes the product of the union as its' focus. Whether creativity is more important in the doing, or in the product, is a matter of personal opinion and varies, not only with ourselves, but also with the subject in question. For instance, take something like painting a picture. For someone with no known talent to pick up a brush and give painting a try, the merit is in the creation, and probably not in the result. For an accomplished, perhaps jaded, artist, the merit may not so much be in the doing as in the result, potentially bringing pleasure to many who will see the result. This is of course a rather silly example and the conclusion must ultimately be subjective.

From Earth, with its inherent fertility, comes the other side of the coin; death and it is within this double-sided element that one meets their fears of the death, rest and re-birth cycle and starts to experience energies. Our bodies often become aware of the changing pulse of life and respond accordingly. In the light months we plan and then grow our ideas and participate fully in our creations. In the dark months we begin to form ideas and meditate deeply and have great thoughts (or so we hope!). A great many of us have a need to hibernate during the dark months, and to look within. The symbol used in the Element of Earth is the stone. (Different people use different symbols or the same symbols assigned to different elements and of course, the ones I am using are a product of my own preference.) An anchor stone, a Touchstone, is frequently used as an image in the meditation Grove and the images of all that is stone include those of aeons of time, patience, stoicism, fortitude and possibly a 'nothingness'. But stones have energies and in their timelessness, seemingly unaware of past, present or future, there is a lesson for us all. Those things which through time we have considered passive, we now find to be actively getting on with its life. Those things we once heard are now listened to, those things accepted may be tolerated, that which was listened to with sympathy now fills us with compassion; there is an active ingredient in our perception which might be considered 'awareness'.

A good example of changing awareness and the use of time is sitting within the meditation grove and meeting one's past or future self. Here are some strange energies, where the past can be experienced as a denser, slower vibration, the present as 'normal' and the future as 'finer' and 'lighter'; unencumbered by the apparent linear passage of time between 'now' and 'then'. All things can be experienced in the eternal 'now' of the Grove and there is much to be learnt from the experience. Consider how much lighter the 'future' can be, until experience colours it accordingly and thereby making it the present. The vibration of that experienced as 'future' is already pre-determined to some degree as is our life potential by karma. Our future, personally or globally is pre-determined to some degree by what has gone before, our social debt incurred and such things as our intent for particular focus in life. From then on it is up to us in the present to weave the tapestry of the future. Not only is it something of an (inner) eye opener to experience one's own vibrational rate but it makes one very aware of the necessity of creating a beautiful tapestry now for later and understanding how attitudes change and therefore the need to move on.

We are not the people of the past; we are of the Now. We may be those very Celts, incarnated, returned again and bearing traces of those times. Perhaps we can bring forward the best of these trends and learn how to use them in the Now. To remember someone or something is to give it energy and it remains 'alive'. Love of land and seeing the spirit flow through it is a good place to start remembering our Celtic past, bringing their passion for the land to the Now with the future in mind. When the Celts worked their way across Europe, sacking Rome, they were unable to comprehend the idols they found there, their concept of deity was in the woods, the water and the land itself; they need no icons. Perhaps the fundamental love of land - whatever our religious persuasion - would do more for our planet than all the talking and posturing. It is not something that can be taught, only experienced, felt within and ultimately threaded through life (eco-friendly products are bought for cleaning purposes, organic foods and clothes purchased, the car left at home, recycling done as standard ....).

If as individuals we 'do our bit' and persevere with our efforts, we can make a difference on a national level. The difference will be noticed by the producers and with the co-operation of the big companies (however grudging) our actions can lead to a better use of land and her creations. Similarly, those things of the past with which we would no longer agree can be remembered and lessons learned, rather than our having to re-experience them again to bring them to the forefront of our consciousness.

Times change and we move on, personally and culturally. For example, the Celts had a high regard for death in battle. They also revered the head as being a major site of energy within the body, the Pendragon - the head of the dragon. Therefore in battle the head of a worthy foe became a trophy. It is possible that the famous Cerne Abbas Giant in Dorset may be carrying a severed head. Carved into a steep hill he would have appeared a ferocious and imposing foe as God to the local area serving to undermine any would-be attackers' moral. But whether or not he is carrying a head, or even if he is of antiquity, he illustrates what we might consider to be the barbaric flavour of the Celtic world. We would like to think we have moved on since this era and would now consider his behaviour unacceptable!

So how do we differentiate between what should be remembered and kept current and what should be remembered but considered inappropriate in the Now? The answer can be found in the Elements - a flow personified by Epona, the Horse Goddess, beloved of the Celts. (Epona was symbolic of wealth for the Celts and represented movement and flow.) In Earth we deal with conception and death as first and last base in our earthly round but we need to experience the other Elements between the two before we can judge what we should retain and what should be consigned to the past. We need to fly out and experience life remembering that today is tomorrow's past; will our current life also be considered by some as 'short and brutish' or as cultured and responsible with love for our land? Wisdom cannot be taught, but hopefully develops with age, experience or memory.

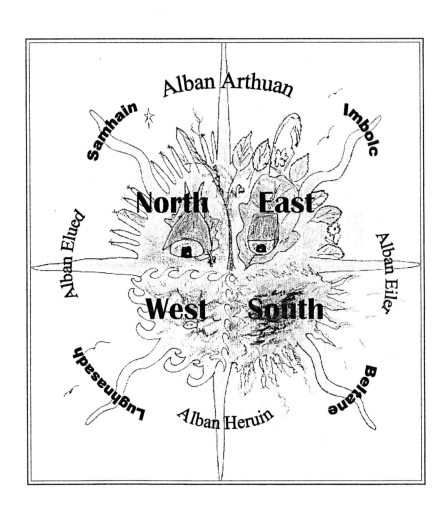

AIR

EAST - AIR

An Air sign first and foremost, I have had to learn the practicalities of life and gently feel my way through the other Elements. It may not be the best place to begin a study of Druidry for experience and learning may well be better started from a supportive Earth Grove, but I came to Druidry to learn whatever I could with a background of trusting in my Gods and a belief in the benefits of meditation. Meditation is for me, something born of the Air and from the East, a chance to fly away, to an arguably more 'real' world, and if this sounds a bit too 'airy', if over-worked it can be. It is a respite from a busy world; a discipline which had to be learnt but a pleasure exceeding all need for substances and with no unpleasant side effects - unless you consider peace and calm a bad thing! Air is my element and if not for my background, where earthbound practicality is absolutely necessary, I would spend far too much of my life day-dreaming and living in my mind. This is the double sided coin for someone born under the influence of Air - vision at its best but with a tendency to over-swing into becoming a dreamer with no handle on life or practical experience of earthly matters.

The Element of Air is all that is Spring. It is the colour of the snowdrop and the gradual emergence of primroses and daffodils, the ethereal pastel shades of the first dawn. It is fragile and newly awakened. The fragrances of these flowers are still green from the proximity of earth. Everything is delicate and fragile; it is the beginning - not conception for that came from Earth, but of actuality. This is the first sign of life slowly strengthening and becoming brighter, endowed with a quality of light so pale and pure as to appear insig-

Men Sryfa, Cornwall

nificant compared to the fire which follows: but it is tough and needs to be.

Trust re-emerges in slightly different forms throughout the elements. At the time of Imbolc, the Celtic Fire Festival celebrated at the beginning of February, trust is a simple beauty celebrated by the use of candles and snowdrops - trust in the continuation of life, an emergence of the life force to nourish and trust in the gentle feminine feel of the festival of first spring. For the old peoples it was a time when much of the stored autumn harvest had been eaten and a particularly difficult time was ahead. Even now, with new types of vegetables grown in our ancient soils, there is still very little that can be harvested from the garden and without foreign imports, we too would have little to fall back on. It is the traditional time for sheep to lamb and our ancestors would have supplemented their diet with the ewes milk. What hope and relief to see the first lambs born, to know the first shoots, the first buds and the first singing birds are just ahead.

There is incredible beauty in the first leaves, the incredible softness and vulnerability and the amazing fragile shades of green barely different from the primroses these first leaves follow. Although many trees burst into leaf much later, it is in March that we see those first innocent leaves defying late frosts, and which, only half a year ahead, will have become the tough, resilient and often flamboyant leaves of the Autumn.

Youth is of the East and we can fly away from Earth, into the face of danger, or fly too close to the sun and burn. A child or youth strives for freedom, to reach out into the world and shake off parental yokes - only to rush out and burn their fingers or to simply discover that adulthood is not as free as might have been imagined. However, with relatively few responsibilities, it is a time of comparative freedom.

Leaving the quadrant of Youth and entering that of Power and Prime energy is usually seen to have taken place by our traditional coming-of-age at 21.

Poωer

With the first conception of power, the sap rises and the opportunities become apparently boundless. The apparent magic of Druidry seen, but not sufficiently understood, could be enticing, exciting and dangerous. To someone without a secure grounding in practicalities, ego could swiftly rise to lofty heights and threaten to overwhelm a fragile connection with spirit. Perhaps with Air more than any other sign, there is a need to work with tools to protect, aid and indeed to ground. To go through a simple process of creating a safe space from which to work both physically and in meditation, to set out on foot to the top of a hill, then to sprout wings and fly is exquisite freedom and the Element of Air is the first for exploring freedom.

When you have a few moments quiet in which you are unlikely to be disturbed, try the following guided meditation to experience an impression of the Element which is Air.

> *'Angel of Air,*
> *Holy Messenger of the Earthly Mother,*
> *Enter deep within me,*
> *As the swallow plummets from the sky,*
> *That I may know the secrets of the wind*
> *And the music of the stars.'*

From 'Stepping Stones to a New Understanding' by Anne MacEwen

Whilst sat comfortably in your chair, start to inhale and exhale slowly and with great care. Do not over-breath and become uncomfortable, nor breath unusually slowly; simply breath gently and carefully. Each time you exhale feel your body become slightly heavier and more relaxed and then, holding this feeling, focus on your breathing for a few moments longer. When you are comfortable and relaxed re-read the words quoted above and then read the following paragraphs.

Whilst not moving from the comfort of your chair, you are now going on a journey to the Realm of Air. It is daylight but the sun has not yet risen. In your mind, picture you are walking on a path through an ancient forest. The air is clear and cool and invigorated by the presence of the trees. The trees are old and widely spaced giving each one room to grow to its full potential. Each tree is of considerable age, offering protection and wisdom; this is a place of sanctuary to which you will be able to return at any time to request support or guidance. As you walk slowly along your path between the trees you become aware of birdsong. A blackbird ahead of you calls 'this way' and you walk a little faster toward the sound. You arrive at a little bridge crossing a stream. As you pause on the bridge you become aware of a fish in the stream below you and a hawk overhead. You continue on your journey, slowly climbing a hill out of the forest, following the path through fields of nodding flowers. A sky lark climbs swiftly into the sky, its flight as erratic as its trilling song. You pause a moment to watch the bird and wonder at its mastery of the air.

As you reach the top of the hill you realise you have a great clarity of view in all directions. There is a slight breeze on your face as you turn instinctively to the East. The sky is lit with gentle, pastel colours of pink and peach blending into an ethereal gorm blue overhead. As you stand there, calm, relaxed, the lark and the blackbird stop singing and there is a hush-full waiting. For a moment you pause your breathing but as the sun tips the horizon you breathe again, inhaling the beauty and inspiration of the new day. You feel part of the flow of life, part of the continuous hope of the eternal sunrise and joy permeates your body, mind and spirit. You raise your arm in salutation and speak aloud of the beauty and wonder you have been invited to witness.

'Angel of Air, enter my lungs and give the air of life to my whole body.'

You find yourself leaning slightly into the breeze and raising both arms, imagining the feel of the breeze through feathers and how it would feel to wheel and ride the thermals as the hawk.

The sun leaves the horizon and sets out across the sky. You take another deep breath and raising your arm one more time in praise and farewell, you turn and return down the hill, past the lark who again starts to sing, down to the bridge and across the stream and into the forest. The blackbird has re-commenced his song and you stop a moment longer to hear his perfection of voice, before stepping purposefully back along the forest path and find yourself breathing deeply, sat in your chair once more.

Take a few deep breaths. You may find it helpful to take this opportunity to get up and move around or to drink a few sips of water.

My tutor gave me a feather to take with me in meditation with which to fly and also to protect. In time I assumed a name used in journeying to similarly protect. I had always found assumed names to be somewhat fanciful but in time came to realise that there is a lot of power in a name and to change one's vibration by the use of a word can lead to a change of power. Lighting a candle, putting on a robe, assuming another name, are all rituals by which to access a vibration. It is to access a changed vibration that a specific route is followed in visualisation, perhaps over a bridge, crossing water and into the Otherworld. However the same route should be used by which to return to full consciousness and awareness of the room or place in which one is physically sat thereby securing one's hold on reality whilst seeking to crossing the boundaries between the seen and unseen worlds.

It did not take long from first starting the Ovate Grade to discover an affinity for the Rowan tree (Mountain Ash) and only a little research revealed it to be an entirely appropriate vibration with which to work; it was not so much my choice of journey-name as the choice that was made for me whilst journeying (by happy 'chance' I also discovered it to be the tree assigned to the immediate period around my birthday in the Michael Vescoli Calendar). The Rowan is a tree for protection, not in the sense of the Oak which offers solid, durable protection in the sense of a heavy, secure door keeping out intruders (and may be the origin of the word 'door'), but in the sense of magical protection. It is fine and free but as tough as old boots given a good rooting. When it bursts its' tight little buds in spring the whole experience of Rowan breaks forth - the buds contain both leaves and blossoms which swiftly swell and progress through the summer to a beauty and ripeness of berry which feeds the birds in the autumn. As the leaves grow old and fall, the sap declines and there is a brief period of rest. It is very early in the following year that the first tight buds can be seen pushing through into the new year and seeking the first sun's warmth and light; it has the youth, energy and magic of the East.

Air is of course breath, something with which our current society has an increasing problem with. With more and more asthma, hay fever and other breathing related illness, we rarely seem to have the ability or inclination to inhale or exhale in the way nature intended. Without breath we are without our connection to life itself. Without breath we cannot articulate our thoughts and desires. We be-little the Element of Air when we speak falsely or babble on with no clarity of particular point and we say that someone is 'full of hot air' or a 'wind-bag'. The clarity of Air turns to a dismal fog, our attention wanders and we 'drift off'. But it is through Air that I find the Awen, the flowing breath of spirit which energises me; whether found through simple ceremony, watching a sunrise or listening to a beautiful piece of music, it is the life force filling every space within every cell. For other people it may come by another route but I am of the Air, this is my home element and I find it here. In ceremony we might speak a phrase three times - many things come in threes in Druidry. This repeat crosses our conscious, sub-conscious and expanded conscious minds, focusing our attention and allowing changes to manifest at the most appropriate level. Whereas power can be built with a carefully repeated intonation such as the Awen, a clap following a request or avowal, can 'fix' the energy of the request.

The *Celestine Prophecy* books tell of shifting energy around within an assembled group of people so that each person in the group receives energy enabling them to express their thoughts clearly and concisely, possibly even beyond what they thought they knew. With careful focus it is indeed possible to send energy to group members and observe them surprise themselves with their sudden ability to express their ideas so ably. Equally it is possible to stand on a power point of earth energy and as the energy flows through one's body, thoughts coalesce and can be made manifest as clear speech.

East is the place on the wheel which includes youth, the Spring and impetuosity, not as in the element of fire where there is drive and flamboyant verve, but a 'head in the clouds' impetuosity with no basis in practicality. As the first element (other than the conception from Earth) there is no background, no experience and this has yet to be learned, to be balanced out by the other elements. Visualisation is rarely a problem for Air signs but a vivid imagination can lead to serious doubt as to the validity of an experience. The answer is found later in an inner 'knowing', a 'feeling', intuition born of the element of earth or the wisdom of the west; and trust.

The typical Air sign can be incisive and the symbol widely used for the Element of Air is the spear indicating swift speed and 'getting straight to the point', mentally acute to the extreme (and sometimes is), in this world but sometimes not actually part of it. We live in the mind, perhaps not noticing those things around us which should be attended to, and create problems for ourselves born of too much thought on a subject which did not perhaps warrant such over-commitment of time. We tend to speak quickly and think fast, leaving other signs wondering what we are about.

Sometimes Air signs lack depth or a quick wit can be at others' expense. As a stereotype Libran I tend to be indecisive, spending a great deal of time seeing all points of the argument and trying to be fair to everyone. To a Fire sign for example, these characteristics are merely time-wasting when I could have been right at the heart of the situation taking action. However, although most people express one element more than another, we all, hopefully, learn to integrate some aspect of the others within ourselves, if only the wisdom from the west and north with the passage of time.

Air has a shimmering quality of vibration, represented by the hawk and shares with fire both light and enlightenment. It is rising to greet the sun and finding a whole new way of viewing a subject; it is about ideas; it is Gorm. Gorm is the colour blue, or perhaps green, sky at dawn, the colour of clear vision. (Think of someone being described as 'gormless' -

without gorm - and turn it to its opposite which is quite beautiful).

When a student first starts the Druid Course, he or she enters the Bardic Grade. The four elements are studied and the use of both sides of the brain instigated. Creativity is considered to be of the right brain and is a balance to the more masculine feel of the analytical, linear and calculating left brain. The historical Bards were raconteurs of tales and lineage, in later years became more minstrel and less overtly Druid: modern Bards are encouraged to awaken an inner creative light through music, prose, verse, writing their own diary of their experiences of the Course, to take up a craft and make their tools for their journeying through the Course for physical use or to call upon for spiritual use. Some students might take up silversmithing, drumming, painting or any number of possibilities. This creativity can be seen to be connected with fertility - something which is frequently misunderstood and the subtlety of point lost almost entirely. But it is not to express an opposite such as use of right or left brain to the exclusion of the other, so much as to experience alternatives that leads to a more complete view. It is about hearing those first whispers of intuition and opening new channels to understanding - but this gentle and creative side of the brain is not weak or ineffectual.

The Winds of Change

A small breeze on a summer's day with the power of a hurricane: I find intuition through the element of Earth but from the element of Air I hear a gentle whisper.

Purchasing my little house was a giant step into the East: I was fully of hope and joy in starting out on my own, a chance to have my own space and work to my own time, but from a material viewpoint it was a great challenge to the point of being very foolish indeed. I was almost daily being faced with potential redundancy at work and the salary was at best basic. I had had a lifetime of living frugally but this was a time I would not wish to repeat. For two years I worked to a system of accounting that few people would consider; I went almost nowhere and did nothing that cost me money, what I ate was largely grown, what was needed for the house, I made, recycled or did without. By the time two years had passed, the novelty had worn off and slowly the lack of means began to suffocate me. My quest for spirit slowed to a standstill when it should have been a time to turn to what I believed in. My financial situation became dire and then one evening I had a life-changing moment.

For two years I had used my weekly allocation of money almost to the penny and to have taken more would have meant stepping onto the slippery slope to losing my house. On the evening in question I had 6p left in my purse; I had no other money at all and it was my lowest point. I had a bath, relaxed a little and inadvertently fell into a oracle-receptive state. A voice spoke to me. It spoke to me with a clarity that touched my soul. It spoke in the form of a question, asking me what I thought I would gain if I had more money. My reaction was violent and shook me to the core - more so than the question. Nothing - I would gain nothing by having more. The 6p represented the amount left having paid the current bills and bought a little food. To worry about more food or a potential problem with the car was in the future, or perhaps not even likely to occur at all in the case of the car. To worry about something that might never happen was an incredible waste of my energies.

It was a truly oracular experience, the words used were not those I would use in my general vocabulary and they were powerful in their simplicity, penetrating to the innermost reaches of my being. I sat to meditate on the question posed to me and apart from a certain need for financial security I could neither fault the logic or dispute my answer. Over the next few weeks I again resumed a spiritual path based on the love I had felt to have been shown to me. The voice was something outside of my conscious self - someone had bothered enough about me to make the effort to communicate with me and provide me with a feeling of support. A voice like that can be trusted, a voice like that inspires reciprocated love.

I can truthfully say that I have not spent time worrying about money since. Certainly for some while afterwards, money was still as hard to come by, but gradually and gently, things improved in the form of an extremely slow-moving but upward and outward spiral. Most importantly, I had no more fear for my financial future.

Many people have oracular experiences - often in the form of a dream. Some dreams seem to have something special about them, a certain quality. It helps to write down a dream, not just as a reminder, but to sort out the meaning. To write out a brief version of the dream clarifies it by taking out any extraneous images.

One night I dreamed of going to a railway station with a number of my peer group from school. They were all going to a performance - to enact a drama -while I was going on a different journey, along a different track (how very true for without exception they have done the marriage and children thing, which was not something I needed or wanted to do). I can re-play the imagery in my mind even now as is often the way with significant dreams, but to write down the words brings its basic meaning into every-day life.

Dream imagery captures an element of life in metaphor and I find it incredible how the basic image is built into a panoramic picture. However, it can also be so directional, to the point of farce, that we cannot possibly miss the issue. The first time I went on holiday abroad I went with friends from school to Austria and became ill almost immediately due to something as simple as having cleaned my teeth in polluted water on the ferry. After several days I became seriously ill, but in my endeavour to not miss a moment of my holiday or to ruin my friends' holiday I learnt a lot about mind over matter. I also became dehydrated and exhausted. On a day when we had no planned trips I sent my friends off for a walk and took the opportunity to rest and soon fell asleep. I found myself walking along a station platform and stop to wait for a train to come in. I glanced up at the name; I was standing on 'Eternity Station'. My mother walked towards me and pointing up at the nameplate said she would never forgive me if I took the train. I decided not to leave - and awoke from the dream with every intention of forcing food and water down my throat until better. What a ridiculous dream - Eternity Station! I was ill but not actually at death's door, and my mother would certainly not threaten me, but the imagery is an excellent example of a meaningful dream and scarcely needs explanation; it worked!

It is possible, with intent and initially a certain amount of 'luck', to change the content of a dream. By remaining in a dream-like state, barely awake, the dream which is still nearby can be re-played and the ending changed or any other part altered to give a different outcome. It seems that in 'falling' asleep one expands outwards in the same manner that in meditation one can travel down and inwards and fly free, upwards and outwards. It is equally possible to be experiencing a dream in 'normal' sleep when a change of apparent reality becomes possible.

Clearly it is possible to change or challenge 'reality' in a number of different states of consciousness; we do it all the time by the use of psychology to influence other people as we present ourselves in a manner in which we wish to be seen. How far does this 'reality' management extend to our conscious lives? For example, are we living a life of apparent poverty for no other reason than that it is the reality which is currently playing and that it need not be the reality if we chose not to 'live' it. The problem is in changing our role and fulfilling our (karmic?) potential in the manner in which we had perhaps 'originally' intended. Is there a distinction or are we precisely where we should be? If the latter, then why can we change any part of our reality, be it that we might call it a 'dream' state? Some of our reality can be recreated by something as simple (or as complicated) as our attitude. Is life itself a product of our mind? Are we all children of the wind seemingly blown along by strange gusts, whirling in some obscure and irrelevant eddy, or can we opt out of being windswept and experience riding a thermal, or dwelling in a caressing zephyr?

Chance Meetings

Another phenomenon I see as blowing on a gentle breeze is coincidence which has become a cornerstone for my belief system. If there is someone prepared to help me, to care, then I am prepared to put my trust in them for I have never come to harm through following advice proffered or through the receipt of gifts offered; I readily accept I know little and often need guidance! The Celestine Prophecy books illustrate the phenomenon of coincidence to good effect and the Experiential Guides which go with them are excellent.

Some coincidences are based on a long term plan orchestrated with beautiful precision and so convoluted that it surely is beyond the realms of belief if viewed purely as 'chance'. In the first year of 'A' Levels at school all students were expected to produce a Thesis. Already being interested in food for health, what the body needs for the proper working of all our component parts and why, I decided to investigate the properties of honey. I also decided that as well as giving the people who marked the Thesis something to think about I wanted to give them something to sample. We had a new neighbour move in who had a bee hive and I thought I would enquire if it would be possible to purchase a tiny piece of comb. I had already met him on a number of occasions for I had to walk about half a mile to the school bus each morning and on wet days he had stopped and kindly offered me a lift - I knew it was him because he had a new white Citroen car which I had seen come out of their drive. Anyhow, I went to his house and knocked on the door. A gentleman answered and I asked to speak to Mr C. - he said I was. Ahhh! Who was the man who had been giving me a lift to the bus stop? I requested a piece of honeycomb with great embarrassment and got out as soon as I could.

A few days later it rained heavily and with considerable trepidation I accepted the offered lift from the stranger. My mother turned super-sleuth and charged into the village butcher's to ask if they knew who the man in the car was. I'm sure they thought her most eccentric but told her he was the local Architect and he lived nearby. He sounded 'reputable' and I continued accepting a lift.

In my last year of 'A' Levels at school I planned to start job hunting and bought what I expected to be the first of many local newspapers. It was to be the only newspaper I bought. There was one secretarial job advertised - for the Architect's office. I got the job and had the pleasure of working for the Architect for five years, when he retired.

I would never have accepted a lift if I hadn't thought he was our new neighbour and they were the only two people I ever came across with that particular model and colour car. The coincidence had had to start nearly two years before I got the job. The subtlety of orchestration is akin to the incredible complexities of karma and if viewed as a loving plan in which every one of us is in the best place at the best time for the best education in life, the organisation is awesome. Imagine all the meetings we would require just to organise the basics of offering someone a job two years ahead, let alone the intricacies of deliberately building in some necessary 'mistakes' to activate the plan.

Most everyone has experienced the sort of coincidence where you meet someone you haven't seen for ages at some remote place miles from home. I've met relatives at Waterloo station and a friend from an evening class on the ferry home from Ireland; this is not uncommon and is usually put down to 'small world' syndrome. Sometimes however the most trivial of 'chance' meeting can prove to be a small cog in someone else's very complex wheel.

The three of us were on holiday in Cornwall and on the evening of the Summer Solstice we planned what we wanted to do and set off in the car. We passed Madron Well and although not part of our plan we unanimously agreed to stop and walk up to the Well.

As we approached the little Baptistry we could hear voices and in view of our first experience there we wondered what we were going to find. The voices stopped, we collectively took a deep breath and stepped pseudo-confidently into the ruins of the little building. Over a dozen anxious faces turned to look at us. 'Hello' said Mum with an encouraging smile. All the faces registered relief and everyone beamed back. The group had travelled from Denver on a tour of our sacred sites and had recently come from watching the sunrise at Glastonbury where they had had a bad experience and made to feel very unwelcome by a party of youths in the town. On their way to Sennen for the night they had come across the sign to the Well and decided to sit in meditation to try to put the experience of the morning behind them. Just prior to our arrival one of the group received an intuitive oracle that someone would come who would be of assistance to them - and in we walked. We were very happy to meet them and offered to lead a convoy of cars to several of the nearby sacred sites.

We all had a wonderful evening sharing ideas and stories; there is very little to beat the rush of sharing an interest.

Were we sent? It certainly had not been part of our plan to visit the Well - or theirs. Many years ago, humbled by 'coincidence', I sat in meditation and whole-heartedly offered any small service I might be able to offer to those who have a wider view than me. There have since been occasions when I have arrived somewhere at an odd time or said something to someone and found myself stood to one side of myself hearing my voice speak, quite sure the words did not originate with me. My Grandfather collapsed one day and although not a day we would visit we arrived just moments afterwards. Similarly, I went for a walk prior to returning to work one afternoon and arrived outside a shop just after my Grandfather had come out and tripped over.

How can such coincidences happen if they not in some way guided? How can they keep on coming, large or small, so impeccably orchestrated? The very best quality of 'gift' is offered and as I cannot believe in such regular 'chance' there must be a purpose and my personal preference is to see each one as an expression of love to all concerned. The more awareness we display for these gifts the more is given; by increasing our recognition of spirit we enhance the connection. By whom specifically is not something that matters unduly, I could argue that it is my Higher Self, a non-incarnated part of my soul group, Guides, Angels or an aspect of God - but does it matter which? To over-analyse the source somehow misses the point. It works and that is the bottom line. There are those people who will of course say I am deluded - fair enough, that is their opinion to which they are entitled, but equally my experience leads me to believe in some form of caring available to us all if only we would allow it in our lives. It is irrespective of religion or indeed any other factor; spirit by whatever name is not exclusive to any specific group, creed, colour, educational background etc.

Trying Things Out

Not only would some say I am deluded, there are those people, and I know a few, who would say that as I am not part of a Christian Church group, I am playing with fire (innocent), hellfire (ignorant), or working for the Devil (in cahoots). I would not give my time and certainly not my soul to anything that was not implicitly and wholly 'good'. I have never been asked to do anything harmful to another or to do anything of which I do not approve; something which stretches my understanding perhaps, but never against my will. There is only love at the end of this line as far as I am concerned and to connect with it through service or in meditation is bliss. Moments of intense joy and love with lingering aftertones of goodwill, peace and happiness cannot be 'bad'. My body feels rejuvenated after meditation and my soul is content having briefly re-connected with Source and if source should prove to be Satan, a Christianised Pan of ancient times, or in any other way forked of tail or cloven of hoof, I have the utmost respect both for the Pan of myth and for the world of nature spirits etc.

Nor is the opinion based on an absence of having experienced fear, I have, and I am very keen not to repeat the experience. I have no doubt as to the possibility of evil but I cannot see a cloven-hoofed figure bearing a Neptune-style trident, reeking of sulphur, getting past my mother. She has a good grip on reality and whilst understanding there are evil things done, we would no more believe in a vengeful God or an 'all fired-up' demon, than we would go pot-holing: we are both claustrophobic. As often seems to be part of the learning process we went through a time of 'trying out' a number of things but even then we were not inclined to try the ouija board; I would no more touch it now than go pot-holing for a second time.

Thinking back I suspect our Guides were probably over-worked in their care and nurture of us and I have the idea of several doing a job share because it would be too much work for one to manage. Michael Bentine had a cartoon of his Guide being carried off on a stretcher - I suspect there are many cross-eyed, mumbling Guides shuffling around a spiritual ward which has a notice on the door saying 'Overworked and Unappreciated'. But perhaps, because I did once hear something that frightened me beyond anything imaginable, it served as a salutary lesson in meddling in certain areas of darkness.

This is the problem with the 'having a go' phase when people first discover the many and varied alternatives available to them. A few people will inevitably become carried away with their findings having turned away from an old mind-set and become fixated with an apparently new way of life, to the exclusion of bringing any balance into their life. New is not necessarily better or any more the whole answer than were the previously held beliefs. Sometimes people lose perspective and all reasoning and rushing into deep and difficult subjects can lead to crises. Some subjects, such as soul retrieval can be incredibly beneficial in a person's life, but should be undertaken following an apprenticeship of the mind and the sensible use of tools and safe spaces in which to work. To rush into these things fired-up with energy can lead to dark areas of the mind, or anywhere else, rising to the surface to potentially overwhelm the enthusiastic but ill-prepared student.

Another area which seems to gleam enticingly to a student is integration with Gods and other Beings. This, as most anything, is a common-sense issue. Whereas some people deal successfully with Familiars and taking on characteristics of an animal type this should be done with considerable care for one's own safety of person and mind and back-up in the form of an experienced physical support group or not-so-physical Grove Guardians. I have a Guardian of my Ovate Grove; a monkish fellow bearing a striking resemblance to my first employer. He is seldom seen but is there to restrict the passage of visitors to my meditations and the flow of events and experiences through them.

When I started the Ovate Grade I slowly built upon my Grove for the Grade, which became strong and vigorous, and I became increasingly aware of a lady asleep within a Quoit. Although not part of the Course it was obvious to me that I needed to work with her and over many, many meditations she stirred, awoke, sat up and finally left her stone casing. She was incredibly lovely and in time I came to trust her wisdom. She was fine and ethereal and of the realms of light. After still more time had passed I was going through a tough patch and whenever I meditated I found the Grove becoming increasingly leafless and barren. One day I found my Grove floor sodden with my blood. It was time to sort myself out and my Lady was an inspiration, a symbol of purity and I came to see that part of her was me in awakened form. Eventually I managed to stem the flow of blood from my heart centre and as the Grove became leafy again and even stronger than before, my Lady and I somehow integrated. Whilst separate and distinct we are also a part of the other and which makes me stronger and empowered. With the recognition of her/myself and the eventual integration of this part of myself within my daily awareness, it was me who had awakened.

Seeking Catherine

To the east, in Dorset, there is a sacred hill, Chapel Hill, which with its little church, is reminiscent of Glastonbury Tor rising out of its wetlands. Abbotsbury is the village at the foot of the hill and is famous for its ancient Swannery. The hill has that certain indefinable something demanding attention, and it is one of those places which a body leaves suffused with energy. The energy here is different to the Michael and Mary earth energy lines, or the Merlin and Morgana lines, with which I am most familiar. Both pairs of lines flow through

Cornwall across the West Country and each pair has their own 'feel' and their own individual vibration. The distinctive Michael energy inspires me to reach out to maintain contact with the flowing spirit about and within me. The Morgana line of the other pair, fills me with an active happiness, and the energy which flows through this beautiful part of Dorset gives me something similar but yet subtly different; it has a signature of flowing contentment. A great deal has been written about the two pairs of lines and several books are suggested at the back of this book. I have not come across any material on the Catherine line although I am quite sure it is a recognised energy, and is probably well documented somewhere. Not being particularly interested in limiting straight lines the earth energies' sinuous flow about a given line of direction appeals to my nature. They undulate across the surface of our earth finding their own contours, reaching up to the craggy places and twisting and turning in serpentine or dragonish loops along river banks to springs, waxing and waning in width and depth and following no apparent specifics other than their own particular whim.

The first time Mum and I deliberately went in search of the Catherine line we little realised we had started with an almost impossibly difficult first-timers' project but we were inspired and full of hope; with hindsight I realise we were dowsing in the vibration of the East.

We tracked a line from the Church on the hill to the village Church which having entered the Church at the donation box, crossed to the South wall and left at the St Catherine window. We noted a single line of dragon tiles near the altar, heading toward the window and then found another energy line coming in from the ancient hill fort direction, glancing across the Church to concentrate at the St Andrew part of the same window. We began to feel uneasy for it all seemed too simple. We crossed back toward the Church on the hill yet again and succeeded in upsetting the small flock of geese by the Tithe

Part of the St Catherine window, Abbostbury

Barn pond. We long ago discovered that animals tend to dislike being pointed at and so with both rods blazing held them at bay, until stupidly I thought I had won them over, turned my back to walk away and was dealt a swift blow to the back of my knee - I could almost hear the goose hissing in indignation 'It's rude to point! Having no further indication of the 'Andrew' line we returned to the hill and quickly found another energy briefly running parallel to the Catherine line. We traced this particularly undulating line back to the village Church (via the wretched geese!). The new line twisted and turned around the Tithe Barn in alarming fashion and suddenly ran into the Church, whizzed round to pay a quick visit to the Catherine window and back out opposite to the entry point. The third section of the window is dedicated to St Nicholas after whom the Church was named.

By now it had been a long morning and we decided to walk down towards the Swannery to sort out our thoughts and eat our sandwiches. There is a patch of grass by the side of the stream near the Swannery where we often picnic and had often remarked on its particular beauty. There is a magnificent tree growing there, the grass has an incredible greenness and there is a patch of Devon violets which flower for many months. After a few moments of munching it occurred to us that we always felt well there and could feel the tell-tale signs of excitement in our solar plexus. We had found a fourth line and this one was distinctly 'feminine'. Close to mental overload, we were unable to accept any more new information that day, so decided not to investigate this further.

Our 'Nicholas', 'Andrew' and 'Catherine' energies all flowed from the Church window toward the East. There are a number of wonderful ancient sites up on the hills nearby and we hoped that at least one of our lines would go to the Hell Stone.

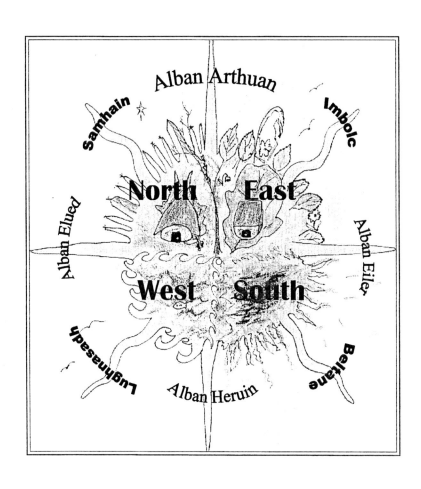

FIRE

SOUTH - FIRE

Shine a light on a crystal and all sides light up; I think we do the same. Sunlight makes us happy. Warmth makes us content. It is the time of greatest strength and courage; our prime time. It is the kundalini rising.

Without light there would be no visible flame from fire. Without light we would see nothing, without spiritual light we would feel nothing to inspire us, without the flame of life within us we are clay. We have words, a great many being interchangeable for the action of sunlight on the physical body and that of a spiritual nature on the soul; light, heat, warmth, spark, fire. South is the Quadrant allocated to the Spiritual aspect of Man and is often recognised as the more distant, patriarchal sun of a number of cultures.

It is, in general, the least understood of the four elements and the one with which most students seem to struggle. I knew the words and literal meanings to express South but could not feel that expression so profoundly inside me in the same way as with the other three elements. It seemed that spirit was too distant to find here. I set out to learn more and requested oracles to point me in the right direction.

Light
A good place to continue my quest for a better understanding was with the ultimate experiences of light and fire combined; in the sunrise and sunset. Each one has its own power, its own beauty and its own expression. For me, sunset's art touches the soul; sunrise's magic engages the spirit.

Roche Rock, Cornwall

To greet the sunrise is a primeval need, going against our modern-day inclination of getting up in the morning as late as possible and scrawling into work a moment before the deadline for appearance. Ask someone on Glastonbury Tor at the Summer Solstice why they got up at 3am to travel there, climb the Tor before breakfast, all to watch the sun rise - which is after all a daily occurrence - and they would probably not be able to give a reasonable or logical answer.

The answer, if one is ventured, would be whimsical, even foolish, to do with greeting the sun, of connecting with the cycle of the seasons and the wheel of life, with being part of the land and all of existence. There would probably be some arm-waving, a somewhat shame-faced expression and a total inability to communicate a logical reasoning processes - but the reason lives inside those who attend.

Sunrise on the longest day rises in the quadrant of the Air and on the shortest day rises in the quadrant of Fire. At the two Equinoxes, those two times of the year when darkness and light are equal, sunrise is in the East; a point of perfect balance. Similarly sunset, depending on the time of year, falls within two quadrants, West and North, dealing with increasing wisdom and age. Our Ancestors sought to build these significant days into their landscape, building stone structures to align with these key dates and even creating barrows, such as Ireland's New Grange, which permit the passage of a shaft of light deep into their interior on a particular day.

There is just something about a sunrise and there is an indefinable something about a specific sunrise; a winter solstice sunrise has an entirely different feel to a summer solstice sunrise. There is a quality of light in those first few moments of sunrise difficult to express in words but felt and held inside one's person. There is a connection of spirit with Source - whatever we might believe it to be, or even if we believe anything at all. And of course, sunrise is a perennial sign of hope; a perpetual new beginning.

The first time my parents and I went to Glastonbury to greet the sun on Alban Heruin, the Summer Solstice, there were comparatively few people making their way to the top as opposed to the crowds that make their pilgrimage now. We were particularly blessed that year. The low-lying mist covered Glastonbury and its environs like a flowing sea. We stood and waited on the 'island' above the mist like survivors of some cataclysm. We looked down onto the rolling, flowing surface. Someone played a flute, another had a small silver bell - it was pure magic, an enchanted isle of people of all nationalities, religious beliefs etc, all in total accord. At the exact moment of sunrise the mist started to flow towards the sun, rolling to the east pulled by a strange magnetism. The mist which was behind us as we stood facing East, flowed past us on the Tor and just simply vanished. Everyone smiled, faces glowing, reflecting the light, happy and in communion with the experience of receiving the light. Soon, hushed expectation became a gentle murmur as people shared a few whispered thoughts and by the time the sun was high and the mist gone, the enchantment had also rolled away and the work of the day began.

The sunrise experience on the Tor has changed over the years and now there is a heavy Police presence - but it is still magical. Part of the experience is the sense of community amongst so many people. Glastonbury is changing its vibration - or are we changing it? Avebury is an incredible centre of the past but Glastonbury has a growing feeling of relevance to now. We are making it what it is and it reflects back to us the vibration we are putting in. Cultures change, epochs of time change with their own relevance to their particular time and it seems to me that as we head into the Age of Aquarius, Glastonbury is becoming a centre of the Age. Avebury has a timeless quality that will always be relevant as a strand revealing the past but visit Glastonbury and feel the strand we are weaving now. Legend has it that Arthur, following his mortal wounding at the Battle of Camlann was taken to Avalon and from there would return, healed, when the 'time is right'. Is this new current to be found at Glastonbury, and doubtless at many other locations, indicative of the coming of the King; the Bear returned from hibernation?

A number of OBODies had come together at Avebury one Spring Equinox to connect with the past and discuss the Order's future. We had a really interesting day and planned an evening around the stones. It was bitterly cold, and with many of us in white robes we processed into the stones with a beautiful moon pouring her light down upon us. Although supposedly holding a meditation in our hearts and minds I confess my concentration lapsed as I found myself noticing the column of figures in front of me, seemingly floating along like ghosts risen from the grave. The following morning we gathered again at Stonehenge for the sunrise. We filed our way in through the stones and the frost settled upon our multi-layered selves to turn us nearly as white as the grass. As I stood and waited my concentration lapsed again and I thought us mad to be stood there in the intense cold; I almost forgot why we had come, but as the sun rose, I remembered in full measure and the warmth spread through my shivering body.

Although the sun itself gave little warmth on a physical level, it ignited an internal flame. When I started the Druid Course it was a continuation of an existing quest for spirit and I wanted to learn all I could whilst remaining separate from any religious aspect. It became the way in which I lived my life until I encountered the Michael energy from within Fire, and now such a sunrise ceremony fans the flame of my quest for spirit still brighter.

Michael forms a figurehead to my spiritual quest. He sets my soul afire at those high and rocky places in Devon and Cornwall through which the May Day/Michael line runs. He is the Archangel allocated to the South, whose symbol I have only recently discovered to be the ancient depiction of the 'swastika' before it became reversed. Michael is for me, the vibration of Beltane personified; the vibration of experience gained travelling through the quadrant which is Air with the added impetus of a recent injection of Fire.

If healing essences can be made by the action of light on flowers etc in water, would the dew if sipped on May Day morning contain the essence of Beltane? To gather dew is traditional - do we imbibe a little of the fire and light? If sufficient could be collected and preserved and used to treat people suffering, as I did once, from a disassociation with spirit, would the essence of all that is Beltane help a reconnection with the light and warmth of spirit? Why not?

If Michael personifies the vibration which is Beltane, was the vibration born of Beltane and the cycle commenced from that point? Does where we commence the cycle alter the perception of the experiences gained; we all start our lives from different points of the year? In this case, does being born of fire, travelling through water and then 'born' from earth to air and return to fire give a different perspective than the more earthly experience of starting with birth in the North and travelling the circle from this point? But from wherever came the birth of the energy, on some rocky outcrop with the combination of breeze, the light, warmth if I am lucky, rain quite possibly, and the contact with the earth, there is a meeting of elements and the spirit of the line flows through me charging my soul; this is to touch Spirit.

I have a dream. One morning on some lone Tor or wild rocky place I will stand alone to watch the sun rise and at my shoulder will appear the form of a Being, a Great Being, in stature, in bearing and in spirit. Whether or not this Being is known as Michael is immaterial and I am not going to quibble over a name for this is of no import. I know how he will look for I may have seen him before. Many years ago, shortly after commencing meditation 'classes' I experienced an Initiation. It was the sort of experience never forgotten. I met an advanced Being whom, although taking physical form, I was unable to 'behold' clearly because his light was so intense. I found myself kneeling before this Being to be blessed and I knew what I wanted to do with my life, I wanted to re-visit this experience, I wanted to learn, to understand and the journey I had already started was given fuel. I wonder if I have followed Michael many times, over many lives, perhaps even living within the influence of the energy line in different countries - not that it matters, unless previous experiences directly enhances my quest now, for the quest is current and what I do now is the Pathway to the future.

Perceptions

It seems that a definition of Gods and Goddesses is frankly impossible. We seem to have a great need to analyse and pigeon-hole everything and there are some things that cannot be sorted and filed away. A God to someone is a Guardian to another, a Goddess being an energy to someone else. It is impossible to analyse status to conform with everyone's personal requirements. People might have made pilgrimage to a holy well and left offerings for the God/ess of the place in the hope of a cure or advice. Now we might call the energy at the site the 'Spirit of Place' (Genius Loci) but there is a need for a tolerance of expression to allow the passage of spirit; analysis or rigid terminology can effectively block the flow.

Across the Pagan community there is a great need for tolerance, including that of the sheer diversity of deity worshipped. At any Gathering it is very possible there will be people who follow a Norse tradition or make an offering to the

Lady Isis. Many people within the community recognise one or two deities who resonate with something inside themselves or have a more general concept of deity held through birthright such as that through Christianity, Buddhism, Judaism etc. This inner resonance could be attributed to previous experience i.e. a deity worshipped in a previous life, or an energy which seems 'attractive' by virtue of it having ascribed to it a number of specific qualities which we might wish to emulate or specifically call upon.

For my part I have a very loose concept of God which sometimes I refer to in the singular for easiness (or laziness) comprising many different and distinct parts. When I am being more honest I would generally say 'the Gods' to encompass those whom I would acknowledge under any banner ie male or female, neither specifically or somehow both such as those of Thunder or the Four Winds, devas/elementals, *Genius Loci*, any particular Pantheon which might be adhered to and the vibration which is my personal 'resonance' whom I call Michael but who is actually non-specific. Michael is a 'figure-head' and is my spiritual Being of Light. It is 'He' to whom I would bellow for help in a crisis and with whom I share my joys; there is another with whom I would share my hurt and inner pain. Does it matter what terminology is used? I think not; I know what I mean inside when I celebrate the changing seasons and the need to give specific title is incredibly irrelevant. If leaving a little food or a twist of cloth in a tree at a holy well worked once, why should it not work now because we would not necessarily label an energy at a site to be a God/ess?

Even our concepts of the same energy name will differ to someone else's. Our molecular structure is held in place by energy and vibrating at a specific rate, holding us together. If ill-health or shock alters our energetic rate of vibration, our experience is necessarily different to someone without either problem or with their own brand of problem. Perhaps someone who is vegetarian resonates at a different frequency to someone who is not, or to someone on tablets for a medical condition - perhaps even to someone who had garlic the evening before! Therefore, the degree of vibration to which we would like to attain is potentially within our grasp - at least to some degree - and some people might, for instance, perceive a need to clear their bodies, or conscience, of the flesh of other creatures.

It has always interested me how people perceive things in a different manner to others. We know what the colour orange looks like but do we all see the same thing? We are preconditioned that the fruit of the same name is orange so we apply the same conditions to something else and say that it is 'orange'. But is it? Do I see orange in the same way that my mother does? I recognise what I deem an orange vibration and declare it to be orange. If I could see with my mother's eyes would I see it as what I would call blue? Why does the taste of cumin appeal to me but have my father grimacing at its awfulness. Discounting any reincarnation/karmic issues, presumably the simple answer is that there is a 'disharmonious resonance' resulting in his disliking the taste intensely. This subjective resonance at a molecular level also applies to opinions and perceptions of spiritual matters. If someone tells me that in their opinion there is a patriarchal God sitting in judgement upon us, my whole being rejects the opinion as being of a frequency I cannot comprehend; in fact I find the idea abhorrent. Based on what I know, or think I know, my past experience, karmic factors and my own personal preference, it does not fit my particular speed of vibration.

Trust is another example of resonance. How many people would trust someone else's explanation of why they should buy into a certain product and let this vibration into their structure? Mass purchasing of a product advertised on the TV is something the retail companies rely on and temper their advertisements to fit into certain models of selling which appeal to us ie something cute or sold by a sportsman; gimmicks to make us want to buy into the story. But what about the bigger issue? Can this be done with religion? It certainly seems to have been, sometimes sold through fear - another vibration. Can someone believe another person's experience of spirit? I cannot expect you to believe what I have come to believe for my belief system is based on my experience and other sundry factors such as up-bringing. Suppose someone reported seeing a vision Michael on the energy line of the same name at say, Roche Rock. I see no reason why there should not be a sighting and if it was someone I trusted implicitly not to misinform me I might consider it further, but even if I saw him for myself I suspect I would maintain an element of disbelief or try to explain it away as an electrical storm or something easier to compre-hend.

There are those experiences which cannot be doubted and these nearly always need to be experienced on a personal basis - but what about that extra factor that makes us trust someone, or accept an idea? I think it possible that one day I might physically see Michael and perhaps I will because I think it possible. Perhaps it might be in such a manner that even I will not doubt the validity of my experience - I am susceptible to the vibration to begin with- but what makes the experience valid? I can only conclude, lamely perhaps, that it a knowing - an internal alignment of molecules, a resonance of vibration. It is the factor which makes one dream stand out from all the others, one journey in meditation particularly significant, a particular deity or idea suit an individual. The vibration of what has been experienced, or believed, fits the molecular structure or rate of personal vibration like keys into locks; unique locks. We all know we are unique but perhaps we do not realise just how unique we are and yet how susceptible to being blown in the wind.

I trust Michael; because it suits me to do so, the energy fits in with my perception of all that is trustworthy, of high ideals, something to grow toward and worthy of adoration; a vibration, an energy, something of itself and nameless but which glows with the fire of spirit. It is an experience of pure fire, pure light and fulfils my perception of a spiritual frequency - but whether or not I would believe my own eyes if this frequency manifested in the physical is another matter. Seen with inner eyes I can comprehend believing what is seen because I have grown used to trusting this realm but in the physical I would be relying on my physical senses and an input of logic and ego in whose interest it would be to discredit the experience, being of non-physical origin, and therefore potentially a threat to its own existence.

I do not consider myself to be psychic, intuitive perhaps and having no such label under which to commit those 'out of normal' experiences which I have 'apparently' witnessed in the physical, I view them as being extremely suspect and leave me questioning my eyesight, ears or anything else I can blame for mis-functioning. I do not trust myself at this level and harbour many doubts - the perennial Doubting Thomas - but perhaps my experience is far greater on the inner planes than it is in the 'real world'. Perhaps a repetition of events in the physical would lead to a 'normalcy' such as that I find in the Otherworldly realms. The answer will most probably be in the absolute 'right-ness' of the fit of the vibration of what is experienced. Some people are more susceptible (or gullible) to believing than others (also read 'trusting') but the bottom line is that it is a personal conviction of validity.

There is so much that cannot be learned, beyond the basics, and needs to be experienced within one's self. However detailed the instructions given of what to do, or not to do, neither wisdom, nor experience, nor a good Druid can be taught. If something is experienced, say a 'visitation', how can a person convince their logical self that what was seen was valid? Ultimately it is down to a knowledge of the basics, an inner feeling of what is right, occasional recourse to a book or Guide to check on direction, and trust. But can one trust one's own experiences? Even if we can reconcile the logical with the intuitive and tell ourselves we did 'see' something, can we trust this impression? We can know inside that we did experience something, our logical minds can be brought to believe it, but was the experience therefore real? I have slightly poor eyesight and there is a middle distance where, like in *A Midsummer Night's Dream*, I can make every bush a bear. Beyond clear seeing, experience, trust and knowing, what other tools have we got to validate an experience?

It would be easy to conclude that if the experience was one of light, there would be input by the source of the experience to ensure we registered belief - which we can later chose to suspend - but equally it might not be an experience of light, being of the realms of darkness, but be as entirely convincing. I am of the mind that beyond our own interpretation of our part in the experience, and subsequent acceptance or otherwise, a small, final percentage of validity rests with the intent behind the experience. I readily accept that this is not without exception, for we are perfectly capable of believing the utmost rubbish imaginable at times, but if there is an energy which cares for us and seeks our advancement it is not such a large step to consider that the energy might actively seek to bring this about.

If we are prepared to work in the realms of the Otherworld, enhance our connection, co-operate and open ourselves to coincidence, service and the furtherance of our own enlightenment, is it any wonder that we could experience the intended manifestation of a distinct and separate energy. Of course, life-changing experiences occur to those who are not actively questing light and I suspect a great many of these experiences come at a time when a person is in an oracle-receiving state or that the magnitude of intent on the part of the energy blazes through to consciousness; many people having had a 'life-changing' moment do go on to learn more about what they experienced and become proponents of the power of spirit and the realms of the light.

My mother had the fortune to experience 'physical' light with enhanced vision. She saw, whilst in an oracle-receiving state, light broken down into component parts - both as molecules and the whole flowing as a wave. To meditate on light is a beautiful experience. Here is a simple, effective and with practice, powerful exercise.

Sit comfortably, still your mind of all butterfly thoughts by gently pushing away all unwanted thoughts and breathe light into the spaces of the body. Start with the large spaces and continue until the small spaces are filled. Choose a silver, gold, blue or pure white light containing all parts; a particular colour or quality of light will probably come to mind. On the out-breath, picture yourself consolidating the movement of the light through your body and moving on to work to transmute any blockages or areas of ill-health to areas of shining light. Be gentle with yourself; this is a beautiful discipline, not a brush with purgatory. There is no need to over-extend your breath - careful, normal breathing is all that is required. Some areas of the body perhaps experiencing pain or a degree of 'unwellness' may take a long time to fill but gently persevere. When you are bathed in light, enjoy it for a few moments and when you are ready gently return to awareness of your room and your normality.

Power

To meditate is to become aware of power. The power of the mind and far beyond into other realms of existence. Knowing power is empowering of itself and it is often possible to recognise someone aware of their power and their place in the scheme of things by something in their eyes. It is however in the pursuit of power, however spiritual the goal, that ego can make a dramatic entry. Ego is part of our make-up and whilst not 'the bad guy' should be carefully balanced lest it abuse its part and burn out of control. To examine one's own motives under a strong light - making oneself answerable to spirit - keeps the ego in check. Such analysis need not be undertaken under the strong light of the sun. A helpful practice for examination is to stand within one's Grove in meditation in darkness but for the light of the stars and moon.

The night sky sheds a distinctly different light which brings out strange shadows and is a useful alternative to harsh sunlight. The moon's light is of course a reflected light but with the interaction of the moon's own influence it is very much a light of its own. The properties of a single star or planet can be similarly used. If to stand within the moon's light with humility and offer oneself up for examination sounds sacrificial, it is, but if one is trying to work for spirit, it is only an over-extension of ego which is sacrificed. Within the carefully prepared Grove we are safe and can be entirely open - something we rarely are in the light of daytime. Alternatively, I find it useful to call upon my Circle of Seven and leave it to them to 'discuss' my recent progress or otherwise. I known this is another mind-game but is of some value. The participants are not called to judge for they each represent an aspect of my whole self - they do however assess kindly but bluntly and can be used in the form of a de-briefing.

Having power is in finding one's niche in life in the form of trust in one's own Gods or in the right-ness of being alive here and now. It can be in a security of knowing one is 'at home' in a particular land, valley or specific house, it can be a sense of knowing the correct-ness of being within a certain family or tribe, being within a certain religion or group of friends, perhaps doing a particular job of work or hobby, the list is almost endless. It is a matter of attitude to some degree but also a heart-felt love rather more difficult to analyse. Contentment is a sure sign of correct-ness but this can be passive leading to a stagnation of energy - it must flow, it must keep moving, be received and given out in the same manner as we process food. Food gives us energy for the working of the body, it is broken down and the constituent parts assimilated, providing the means for life to flow. The life force itself is within the food adding extra dimension and we are slowly becoming more aware of the need to eat really fresh, and organic food which, without its many and varied contaminants, will contain a less inhibited life force thus allowing an easier passage of energy within us and indeed through us. This flow of life can be seen as a flame - do we burn dully or are we consumed by it? Is it given passage or blocked? Spirit or life force - the same thing or different strands of the same flow of fire?

Below is a guided visualisation incorporating aspects of the Element of Fire tempered by the other elements.

> *The green leaves of the trees*
> *Do worship thee,*
> *And through thee is the tiny wheat kernel*
> *Become a river of golden grass,*
> *Moving with the wind.*
> *Through thee is opened the flower*
> *In the centre of my body.*
> *Therefore will I never hide myself*
> *From thee.*
> *Angel of Sun,*
> *Holy messenger of the Earthly Mother,*
> *Enter the holy temple within me*
> *And give me the Fire of Life.'*

From 'Stepping Stones to a New Understanding' by Anne MacEwen

Sit comfortably in your chair and inhale and exhale gently and carefully feeling your body slowly relax and become slightly heavy. Re-read the quotation above. Take a deep breath and as you slowly exhale, picture energy contained within that breath filling every cell within your body. Spend a few moments visualising this and then picture yourself walking along the path in the ancient woodland. It is midday and the light is shining fully on every tree and each and every one seems to be bathing in the light. You continue your walk and hear a noise. Ahead of you a fully-antlered stag leaps onto the path and halts. He turns his head and looks at you then leaps away out of sight. You are awed by his splendour and hope to catch sight of him again. You come to the little bridge crossing the stream. There is a fish, almost motionless in the water, gently waving its tail to keep itself in position. You notice a chalice left on the bridge which you fill from the stream and take with you on your journey. You climb the hill you travelled before, past the lark still trilling in the clear air and upward to the summit of the hill where the view is limitless. The midday sun is hot but there is a gently breeze to keep you cool. You take a few sips from your chalice of water and sit on the grass cradling it between your hands in your lap.

The sun's light is fierce and as you gently breath in the light and the air you become filled with that light and become gently invigorated. You are inspired to learn more about your purpose and as the light continues to fill you, you become filled with resolve, courage for the quest ahead, protected by the fire within you which you know, used wisely, will sustain you and remain with you for all time.

'Angel of Power, descend upon my Acting Body and direct all my acts'.

You hold the chalice tightly and offer it out toward the sun, then drink the last of the water and stand up to depart. Saluting the sun with one hand you make your way back down the hill, smile a greeting at the familiar lark and return to the bridge. You leave the chalice there for the next pilgrim to take up the hill, but keeping the warmth and vigour inside you, you cross the bridge and make your way back through the ancient woodland. A distant noise catches your attention and you catch a glimpse of the same stag you saw before, leaping away through the trees. Filled with love and life and light you continue along the wooded path until you find yourself once more conscious of being sat in your chair.

Take a deep breath and feel the warmth of the sun's glow inside you. Savour it for a moment longer then go and fetch a drink of water or walk around for a few minutes.

The symbol for South, the Element of Fire, is the sword. If you consider this for a moment, a sword can be used as a symbol of power to either protect and defend or to provoke and attack. It symbolises strength and courage, but it can also be the means by which to wound. Like Excalibur it should be used only in the cause of what is right. Power can be from inside oneself, called upon, exercised or experienced, but it is when it is intentionally exerted over another or intentionally pulled from another that the mis-used power burns darkly. Some people drag energy from others, sapping their strength in vampire-like manner and leaving them feeling drained. In less calculated manner, a couple may have a flow of energy when first they fall in love but when one is no longer prepared to give their energy freely, the other finds their energy source has dried up. Exerting power over others is the potentially worst form of abuse of energy. Employers manage their employees and duties may need to be designated or directed but it is when ego creeps in that energy becomes mis-used.

I find energy in nature; a magnificent tree, a fragile flower, the beauty in a sunrise or sunset, or harness power from the recognition of the qualities of crystal or life itself. This energy keeps me feeling alive and in communication with spirit and in the exchange and flow I hope the communication is a two-way experience. Sometimes communication breaks down through illness creating a block and treatment is required to enable energy to flow so we can be made well again. An increasing number of people are using complementary medicines which can gently and subtly break down a block on the appropriate level. Without illness, without blockage we are lighter, finer, less dense and without the dark areas of blockage we permit the passage of light and electrical impulse into our every cell.

Sometimes the passage of light energy through our bodies can have an intoxicating effect. For instance, to contemplate dew on grass or a ferny foliage acts as a focus to still the mind but also the wonder of the colours and sparkle of light are incredibly inebriating. My mother and I were at Totnes looking out on to the river and watching a sprinkling of autumn leaves carried along by the flow. I found myself gazing at points of shining, iridescent light. At first I saw only green and bronze but the longer I looked the more the colours shone across the colour spectrum. I looked away to clear my focus but as I looked back the leaves still shone. As Mum gazed into the water she too saw the leaves begin to shine. We gazed, entranced, for some considerable time and the leaves shone still more brightly and filled our person with a wonderful power. I was forced to break away as I had to drive home and to stay would have meant becoming drunk on the reflected light. Imagine explaining to the traffic police - 'it was the leaves Officer, honest'!

Having seen such light and experienced the vibration of the colour and sparkle within one's being, it is easy to do a mental search and 'find' the feeling in our memory banks - to write of this intoxication is to call upon it even now - and to 'remember' the vibration of an experience is both another tool to use in journeying or ceremony, and also provides the means for a moment's indulgence and relaxation. Using this 'search' method to invoke or evoke can be used to call upon the properties of the vibration, such as calling upon the Michael energy as perceived to be, for strength, courage and light; to call upon one of the elements or directions; a deity, the vibration of hope or love.

Fire - Rising

Continuing my quest for greater understanding of the meaning of South I sat meditating one evening, inwardly dowsing to catch the vibration which is the essence of fire and pondering on how to light a candle by calling upon the vibration ie without the use of a physical match. Clearly this should be no stage trick for it has great potential for considerable reprisal and I further considered the properties of such a fire; would it burn the person who called upon it and would that person be able to control it? In my mind, very clearly, I saw a creature watching me. Initially it had the appearance of a snake but was clearly more like a lizard: the salamander watched me. If he was the product of my imagination I had no idea I knew how one looked. His look was not dangerous, he was clearly assessing me - he observed me. He was incredibly beautiful. I continued to look at him and he read me through to my soul. The next move would be his.

A few weeks later I started to experience a fire within my body; inwardly I found myself often seething with a red rage. Whilst outwardly I found myself acting 'normally' and some-times surprised myself by saying and doing and behaving as though nothing was changing, inwardly I boiled. In some small measure my tolerance levels were reduced but mostly I was amazed at my apparent normalcy. The rage inside me continued for several weeks - it was not anger - it was energy. I was not cross or bottling up hate or frustration, it was an influx of fire coming from low down inside of me and burning up through and filling every space of my being. During this time I repeatedly dreamed of twinning serpents and fusion, which I knew to be symbols of serpent energy in the form of the kundalini; fire, power and healing.

As the weeks passed my dreams became farcical. I saw a tail-less plane, without direction, without stability, and realised that although there was no point in my going to a Doctor, for this was not a physical condition to be treated, I was nevertheless in need of some relief of the effects of the power raging through me. Meditation and journeying may have proved a means by which to stop or interrupt the flow but these options were somehow inappropriate and it was necessary for me to go through this. What was required was neither prevention, nor cure, but channelling to give me some rest for body, mind and spirit. I changed my diet slightly and spent hours sat on the seashore listening, and watching the waves roll in, feeling the salt spray on my face and tasting the salt, breathing in the scent of the sea and the negative ions. I gave myself over entirely to the power of the sea and for as long as I stayed near water I had respite from the relentless, ceaseless burning.

Largely with hindsight, several points become apparent. Firstly, that this was non-physical and had to be experienced and not prevented; not allowed to burn out of control, used, not suppressed, for damage could result from such an action; to ignore its presence would have been to miss out on an important experience; the energy came across different levels ie not just physically and so could be tempered by the use of 'opposites'. I did try using my home element of Air to give me respite but I became chilled and the fire raged coldly - not particularly pleasant - and I tried working with Earth but this merely dulled the fire, making it burn sluggishly and sickly.

With time and practice it becomes apparent as to which tool to work with; for instance if healing is required you might choose to visualise drinking from a cup or Grail, to defend yourself you might choose to work with a sword or use a spear or wand for direction etc. No rules can be given for everyone's experience will of course be slightly different, but however used you may be to working with symbols or archetypes from myth or legend, there comes a time when nothing presents itself for use and it is time to seek oracles. Either a physical oracle can be sought or you can opt to journey to seek an ally. In either case you must remain expectantly watchful and if something presents itself to you which is not clearly understood, consider how you feel about it, what it represents and ultimately whether or not you consider it to be wise for there is no law that says you must follow any advice proffered.

Should you receive an oracle in the form of a complicated dream, take a few minutes to condense the dream into a single sentence, thereby taking out all the extraneous images and check for ambiguity in symbols which could be relevant to your situation. If an animal appears but no obvious message, think about what that animal represents and how you can use or relate to this image eg if you see a wolf during a meditation do you see it as a loner, a pack animal, wild, free, savage, brutal .....? Is there a message encoded in the imagery? Or do you need to work with the image of that 'wolf' and journey with him as your guide and ally?

Dowsing in Fire
Our next foray into dowsing was to the ancient sites on the hills around Abbotsbury. We planned our trip with

Mum at the Grey Mare

meticulous care and our first stop was the home-made cake shop in Abbotsbury where we bought pasties and cake. We took it up on the hills to eat it rather than squash it into our jacket pockets (which seemed perfectly justifiable at the time) and then headed toward the stone circle between the Hell Stone and the Grey Mare. Squelching through mud we requested permission to work there and fairly swiftly ascertained that the energy we were calling 'Catherine' was indeed present. We did a swift diagram to illustrate the direction of flow and headed to the Grey Mare and Her Colts - another ancient, sacred site.

We quickly found an entry and exit point for Catherine at the Mare and stumbled across one of the other lines that flowed into the village Church and out of the Andrew part of the stained glass window. This energy went into the mound but did not emerge; we concluded 'he' had gone to ground and would probably re-emerge in the next field which had a 'look' to it (not very scientific, but did actually prove accurate). Mum was stood on the mound logging our results when she observed me to 'light up' and trail a comet tail of light. The more she looked the more she could see and when we dowsed the area on which she was standing we found it to be an energy node. The area was quite small so we took turns to stand there - there's nothing the matter with us! It seems likely that having stood on this incredible energy source we acutely enhanced our perception for once we had started on the next stage, things began to move rather fast.

Our plan was to go on to the Kingston Russell stone circle but first we wanted to find where the line we were calling 'Andrew' surfaced in the field. This was easily done and lit up with energy, fire and enthusiasm we progressed down through the fields dowsing rods blazing. Almost immediately we began to find a twisting, turning, caduceus-style pathway along the hedges toward the stone circle. As Catherine came in, Andrew went out and the pair of them looped and twisted dozens of times along the hedges as far as thirty feet out into the field. We were unable to check if the same happened the other side of the hedge but it seemed very probable. Soon all mapping attempts broke down, and the extent of the caduceus caused us to seriously question our abilities, but we also became increasingly convinced that the energy on the mound was the cause of our prolific findings.

Catherine carefully looped around the small spring in the corner of one of the fields and they both passed, one either side of the gateway, into the next field where they continued to loop. Bogged down in mud and data we couldn't find where the pair stopped looping along the hedge and crossed to and from the circle.

We thought we had experienced the ultimate in data until we started out around the circle. It became so complicated that we drew the circle, I dowsed and Mum mapped it out. The caduceus effect in the hedge did the same thing around the circle. It was clear that some stones had long since vanished but the energies did not recognise their absence. Between every stone, or space, one ran in and in the next space the other went in or out and so this continued all around the

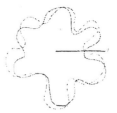

circle, almost faultlessly. One other energy, not previously encountered, crossed to the centre of the circle but like 'Andrew' at the Grey Mare, did not leave it.

We went home mind-blown. Later on that evening Mum and I got out the map to attempt to map-dowse the general direction of the Andrew energy line. It seemed to flow onwards from the Kingston Russell circle to various other significant sites and towards Eggardon Hill, Lewesdon, Pilsdon, Lamberts Castle and to our horror onto our own beacon hill. We were perfectly aware of an energy running across the hill which rises behind my parents house, but had never considered it might be the same one. The energy appeared to travel to Muchelney in Somerset and onward to join into the Michael line somewhere just east of Glastonbury. (On subsequent excursions to follow 'Andrew' the flow of the line varied but to date I am unable to determine the factor which causes the variation, neither have we followed the line into Somerset.)

That night just prior to drifting off to sleep I had another revelation about the energy we had been seeking at Abbotsbury. When I started the Ovate Grade I repeatedly encountered the lovely Lady with whom I finally experienced a sort of integration. I had at an early stage enquired her name and she had said, somewhat enigmatically, something that sounded like 'Amonda', there was a slight pause and then she said 'Catherine'. Surely there could be no link with our line-chasing around Abbotsbury? Logically, it was all too ridiculous, but we have had such strange things happen over the years since we started chasing spirit, it was fair to say that anything was possible. I found myself dwelling on the 'Amonda'. Was it an anagram or form of code? The following day I looked for the word in my turn-of-the-century dictionary. Nothing. It occurred to me (or I was prompted) to reverse the spelling. Incredibly, I discovered an adnomial word is one relating to an adnoun, 'a word preceding a noun' like 'country' cottage.   I have always referred to her as my Lady - not a titular My Lady but as in 'she who is mine'.   She is my Lady Catherine.

The following night I lay there in bed, in an ideal oracle-receiving state, and quickly went through the process of entering my Ovate Grove, calling upon my Lady. By the time I had carried out my short mind-journey and arrived and settled myself to wait in my Ovate Grove, she had arrived. She was happy and sparks were all but flying off her shining self. She had always been serious before but this time she was transformed into a being of gaiety. If this had been physical I would have been open-mouthed. As it was I found myself unable to ask a linear question for my thoughts were looping around like the pair of energies around Kingston Russell stone circle.

Eventually I managed to say how bewildered I was about our apparent findings and needed some help to sort out my thoughts. She asked me how I experienced my much-loved Michael vibration. I said that it was like a through-flow of energy. She smiled and asked 'And the dimension where this is experienced?'
I said 'On a spiritual plane?'
'And the energy you know as Morgana which makes you happy?'
'On the physical' I replied confidently.
'Where - specifically?'

This took some thought but eventually I pictured individual cells in my body. 'In the spaces, within the cells' I replied with a rush of sudden understanding. The effect of the presence of the energy was no doubt throughout my body in the manner of a total flow, but only experienced in the space within individual cells. She asked me to think again about the Michael energy and it came to me in an instant 'In the spaces between the cells'. From her radiance it was clear I had hit on an important truth. I felt at the top of the class!

'And me?' she asked. 'My interaction with you?'

'Somewhere between the two - no, more like Michael. Between the cells but experienced in a different way; from the emotional plane.'

She smiled and withdrew her presence from my Grove. Although I had not received any obvious answers to the mystery of the energies I had a lot to consider. I returned my mind to my room and as I settled to sleep it occurred to me that I had finished dowsing in the South and was on the junction with West.

Spaces, Strands and Positions

Increasingly an awareness of vibration becomes necessary in my quest for Spirit. I remember from Physics lessons at school that molecules are tightly packed for a solid, slightly more open in density for a liquid and quite scattered for a gas. The molecules are 'held' in place in formation, vibrating at a given frequency. This accounts for why we look the way we do, why the mug with the coffee in it looks like it does, or the flower on my desk is as it is with its own particular perfume. But where does the life force reside which separates the mug from my flower? Somewhere in the spaces between the varying packed molecules must flow another energy which separates me from my table and makes me live. We all know that in the dissection of a living thing the life would be lost at some stage, its home never found and the living thing thus proclaimed dead. Life flows through us until such time as the cells breakdown through illness, age or neglect.

Spirit is always available if we are only aware of it and open ourselves to an awareness of it. Is it so very different to the life force itself? A different aspect, always available, capable of filling all people which makes it both limitless and extraordinarily diverse. Perhaps it is not so much a force which flows around us available for us to tune in to, as much of a tuning in to the space between ones own molecules, a recognition of the signal from within: if it is potentially compatible with all people it must be able to cross every preconceived barrier and surely, for so many considerations to be taken into account there is only the one answer, that where else it may also be, it is inside each one of us. Our own energies overflow outside of our apparent physical boundary in what we loosely term the aura. Our auras intermingle, sometimes against our will, sometimes with someone we wouldn't wish to share space, sometimes in such a manner as to cause a friction, or a healing. Sometimes we choose to share our space with other energies such as trees - asking first of course. And sometimes we seek to connect more fully with our spirit energy to enhance our recognition of it within ourselves and heighten our 'life' experience. It is a breath and it is a flame.

Perhaps if this flowing spirit has passed through us and every other thing in the same way, similar to radio waves for instance, it is easier to understand that we are all linked. Some people are natural radio sets and can pick up on the signal in some form and others can not. Some can dowse this signal as a vibration, a frequency and feel, see or hear it as something with which they have a resonance.

If this same force or forces flow through us and the trees, animals, birds and rocks etc this inter-relation might be better understood and that with which we have an affinity might make us more appreciative of it and less likely to destroy it. If we can see the life on our planet as being as connected as we are by energy there follows a Round Table mode of thinking where all species etc are as relevant as each other, of equal value, all of which having something to say and further, something worth listening to. My dictionary tells me that spirit is the 'vital or animating force' and I have said how I experience various energies flowing through me at a cellular level; some outside of the molecule in the spaces between, or within the molecule in the space found there.

And what is the difference between 'life force', the Awen, spirit, energy etc? Aspects of the same thing manifesting at slightly different vibrational rates or separate energies? A person can be comatose with life still flowing through them and upon recovery tell of their spirit being elsewhere although ultimately connected with the comatose body. Does a carrot have all these energies or just some of them? A patch of carrots might well have a helper, a Deva - do we? Is there a human deva or are we each one of us our own devas? If we are, why do we no longer communicate with all the other devas of species? Some people do of course but following the loss of communication for the greater number of us with other devas, we lost the inter-connectedness of ourselves with other life forms. What a loss. Is it any wonder that in that loss of communication, we manifest a loss of understanding and hence perpetrate some distinctly 'un-spiritual' crimes against species.

It is similar within the religions of the world where understanding is lost of another faith. Communication dries up, each sees its own expression of spirit to be unique in its 'right-ness' and evil perpetrated in its' name - the very antithesis to flowing spirit. The Round Table is banished and a wasteland ensues. We live in a world where greater tolerance is called for in the workplace or within the community but yet we become increasingly more intolerant in other respects. A crying child in a restaurant is glared at and increasingly our own small space becomes inviolate. Our world view as we portray it becomes greater in national tolerance but our personal space becomes smaller in what is acceptable to us. Only relatively few years ago our national tolerance was less and our personal tolerance more. Are we recognising one as distinct from another instead of an inter-connecting whole - separate strands rather than a flowing one-ness? And why do we recognise some parts of society more than another ie our older generation is notoriously unvalued? Our Elders are a strand of life's flowing whole. Why do we seek to separate the strands and lose sight of the whole picture?

Spring comes early here to Devon and in the wide valley where I live the early flowers come very early indeed. Thinking about our growing personal intolerance and whether this was a correlation between this and our apparent lack of appreciation for the manifestation of spirit, I went for a walk. The sun was shining down, warming air and land. Suddenly, for no apparent reason, I tripped, nearly propelling myself into the hedge and coming face-to-face with wild honeysuckle. (Oracles come in many guises). The honeysuckle, the primroses and daffodils, the periwinkles, snapdragons and first pink campions are all part of the glory and freshness of the spring. They are separate but they each have their place and contribute to the whole glory of spring - the difference, as with many things, is in the recognition. To analyse the flowing inspiration of the Awen, to dissect the difference between spirit or life force, is pointless for in the dissection dies the mystery, the beauty and the wonder of it all. Besides, we each of us have our own perspectives and would never agree on a definitive conclusion of results. How can we all agree on what is 'beautiful' let alone what is spirit?

It occurred to me to remember that over-analysis from my home element of Air can lead to a fog. Examination, determination and repeatable experimentation gives credence to many of the ideas put forward giving it a certain qualification, but like all things this can be over-done. We have a need to examine but equally we have a need to understand there is a beauty in a pattern of numbers, artistry in a molecular structure and perfection in the multiplication of cells. We distinguish between science and art, our Elders and a youthful perfection in society, right and wrong but they are strands of their own perfect whole. We need a change of attitude, a recognition of each perfection, a tolerance to all strands and a need to see wholeness not an apparently increasing separatism. We are talking about a universal fire running through all life, not stopping to discriminate, a spirit which flows equally and by which all life comes to the Round Table to say their piece and listen to others. It takes Air to en-vision, fire for energy and strength but it takes the second half of the cycle to see any wisdom gained from the experience to date.

Astrologically the twelve signs is split into four, each being ascribed to Air, Fire, Earth or Water. The three assigned to each element are further categorised as Cardinal, Fixed or Mutable making a most impressive cycle. Traditionally the sun rises in one each of Air, Fire, Earth and Water astrological signs during each of the Solar Festivals. The signs in which it rises are Cardinal signs, those signs most invigorated by the change from the previous Element to its own. The dates on which the Fire Festivals fall are the Fixed signs, those signs best displaying the attributes of the sign in question. In other words, the sun itself uses all the Elements available to it to increase the experience, or ours of it, as it progresses around the wheel of the year. For example at Lughnasadh, the Autumn Fire Festival, the sun is in Leo, a fixed Fire sign and its own ascribed sign. The sun experiences the Element of Fire and it is at this time that the sun blazes brightest and shines down on the ripening corn.

South represents fire in its varying forms and represents a person in the prime of life and at the height of their strength, it is purpose and direct action. The animal symbolising the element of fire is the stag - a magnificent beast who at the height of his power epitomises sexual energy and is the quadrant in which we most frequently raise our children. Beltane is the Fire Festival celebrated within the quadrant when children are conceived and when the stock are driven between the fires out to summer pasture. South is fire in the sense of heat, fire as spirit and as light is visible sunlight or spiritual enlightenment. The light and enlightenment is shared with East but in Fire it can be seen to have a different bias. Light is spiritual, it is sunlight which seeks to fill every conceivable dark space, physical or spiritual; the two are often interchangeable. This is the element nearest to spirit; the element nearest to the finding of the Grail at the end of the Quest. However it is also the element which has the means to burn out of control without the integration of West, East and North. Druidry contains a lot of paradox and an understanding of the power of an opposite is yet one more useful tool to work with.

Let us imagine for a moment that you have cast, and are sitting within, a sacred circle. You are sitting in the South, expressing the qualities of South, facing inwards with the North opposite to your position. Consider the power from the directions to be experienced as a breeze. You are sat in a position of prime strength within the circle and the cool breeze of the qualities of North blowing toward you. The result is a position of passion and fire met by a cooling breeze. Or perhaps you are facing outwards in the South position and the North wind is blowing you onwards further South - carrying you with it ever Southward. The experience is entirely different. You are sat in a position of prime energy and being blown by cool reasoning even further toward flame and passion. What are you intending to express? Do you need to express an element but counteracted at its most extreme by its opposite, or do you need an active opposite pushing you further toward the element you want to express? Active or passive? Moving or building?

Another example. Suppose you are sitting in the West facing East. You are expressing an accumulated wisdom and emotion of the West, with the breeze of the West at your back whilst facing an energy of youthful vigour, eagerness and vision; an excellent place to sit! Or, sit in the West facing outwards expressing west, facing further west with the easterly wind at your back. Blown by enthusiasm you are tempered by your own westerly aspect whilst seeking it even further.

Depending on your intent it is the subtly which is the beauty of using the opposing elements as tools. (Depending on the particular element you express most readily in your life you may already be long gone, in which case extend your reasoning to harness your right brain energy and have another go - you may never use opposing directions as a tool but it is good for the brain to try to understand its relevance!) Compare the following. Imagine yourself sat in the west facing to the east as before. You are expressing wisdom, with wisdom to your back, facing new ideas, vision and inspiration. Now move to sit in the east expressing youthful vigour and inspiration being blown by its energy and meeting the breeze from the west tempering the youthful enthusiasm with wisdom. Would you rather express wisdom enhanced by vision, or youthful enthusiasm tempered by wisdom - subtle, but depending on your purpose, of great value.

Finally, consider yourself to be a spark of light in the centre of your circle, not facing any specific direction, just being present there. All four breezes blow towards you but equally blow with you. You would be held in place by apparently conflicting breezes, at a point of no movement, better described as the eye of a storm; the calm centre within. Each direction can supply a particular influence tempered by its opposite, insight and vision from the East, combining with vigour and passion of the South, tempered by the wisdom of experience from the West and a deep nurturing and hope from the North; this is the point of balance. All burnt out from the effort? The next quadrant is that of Water. The first half of life, of being dreamers and the driven, gives way to the second half of actuality and experience.

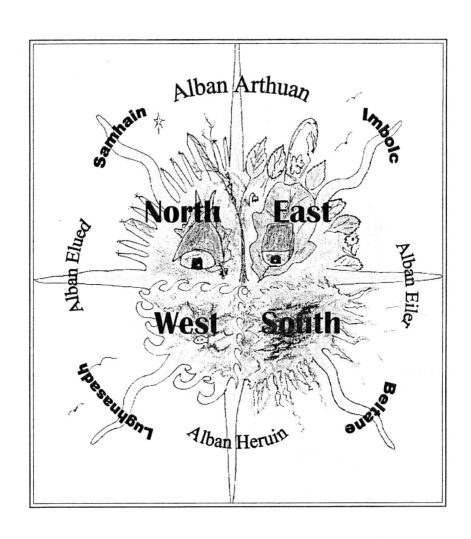

WATER

WEST - WATER

West is the quadrant where the initial dreams have already been dreamed, the fire and enthusiasm of the prime of life experienced and now the lessons from these experiences are being integrated with a growing wisdom born of age. In very general terms if life is seen to 'begin at forty' the West is the period of time from then to the approximate age of retirement.

The colours of Autumn are highly flamboyant, still burning brightly before the first light frost of the forthcoming winter and the Fall. The flowers of the season are amongst the brightest and most flamboyant and the corn is ripening in the field prior to being cutting for food in the winter and seed for the following spring. It is a beautiful time, still light and warm and a time to reap the harvest of whatever was first sown in the Spring of youth. It is a time to rejoice and appreciate what has been learned and still to be enjoyed. There is a stillness, not a passive stillness when outmoded beliefs are clung to from habit, but a time of soul which still flows, analysing and throwing out, but yet forming newly germinated belief systems. There is a movement but yet a stillness born of a point of ebb and flow, a constant motion holding, not clinging; flowing and flowering.

It is a time to learn about the ebb and flow, the high ideals of youth and vigour give way to realistic expectation; the children have grown and there is more time for oneself. We learn to 'hold tightly, let go lightly'.

The Bardic Grade was started in Air with vision and perhaps, unrealistic expectation. The old folk heroes seen to do

Somerset Levels, towards Glastonbury Tor

courageous and daring deeds give way to an understanding of the tale behind the tale. Music, sought in the East, perhaps as a means by which to escape from the increasing realism of practical life, is heard again with more soul, through experience of pain and a learned ability to listen and share both tears of grief and laughter. Soul time. It is an element about emotions and is represented by the symbol of the Chalice or Grail.

'Angel of Water,
Holy Messenger of the Earthly Mother,
Enter the blood that flows through me,
Wash my body in the rain
That falls from heaven
And give me the Water of Life'

From '*Stepping Stones to a New Understanding*' by Anne MacEwen

From your chair, sitting comfortably, slowly inhale and exhale and feel your body becoming relaxed and slightly heavy. Re-read the quotation above and in your mind picture yourself in the ancient forest of protecting and nurturing trees. It is late in the afternoon and the light through the trees is hazy with small gnats circling idly within the lightshafts. There is peace in the forest. You walk along the path between the trees to the bridge. The birds are taking a siesta and all you can hear is the sound of the breeze in the tops of the trees and the burble of the stream nearby. You cross the bridge and turn to your left, following the stream as it makes its way towards the sea some miles distant. You cross a meadow, still following the stream, which starts to widen out and become a river. You find a log beside the water bank, slightly overhung by hazel trees and decide to sit and watch and listen to the stream. A kingfisher darts in splendid turquoise across the stream and you are aware of fish in the stream in the more lazy, deeper pools of the water. Some ripe hazel nuts have fallen beside the log and you reach out for two stones by your feet, crack the nuts and nibble on the sweet kernels. You become aware of how the stream started as a bubbling of water through the earth, gathering to a trickle and wending its way to where you are sitting now and on past you for some distance to eventually join the salt sea. It is a continuous journey containing many experiences. It has forged its own banks and runs sometimes fast and sometimes slowly, over gravel, through fields, giving life to many creatures within it, to those who live on or above it and to those who drink from it. In the late afternoon sun you think about its journey and its many aspects of character.

'Angel of Wisdom, descend upon my Thinking Body and enlighten all my thoughts'.

A sudden 'plop' catches your attention as a fish jumps in the stream. You inhale deeply and stand up. You walk slowly back through the meadow to stand on the bridge and pause to peer into the water and acknowledge the salmon who dwells there. You step off the bridge and walk back through the ancient woodland to find yourself once more, sitting comfortably in your chair. Inhale deeply several times and become aware of your room.

Water is the element assigned to the west. It has many analogies used in the life experience. It is cleansing and on wash day the sheets snap and crack on the washing line as the window blows through them or they are dried under a fiery sun. Water causes the little seed in a state of dormancy to sprout and grow and with the addition of air and fire it can grow into a fine plant. Wisdom is thought of as coming from a deep well of experience, or expressed as a flowing stream; emotions can be expressed as tears; fountains are often used in myth and legend, purveyors of youth or wisdom. We are told molecules comprise protons, electrons, neutrons etc but what is in the space between the 'shell' and all those little whizzing bits? Water? If you put an electrical charge through water you will get a shock. If spirit flows as an impulse through the water within a molecule, perhaps this too can give us a shock; a sudden contact with spirit could be a big shock! This is an element capable of shaking our carefully built foundations.

Facing Challenge

Emotion is energy in motion. Fury, frustration, joy, grief etc are all emotions and can be likened to torrents of water, gentle streams, a stagnant pool, a gentle burble or stifled dam. It can be exhilarating to ride the whitewater but to turn and face the current, or as King Canute, demand a halt to the tide, one risks obliteration. Water is life and this element can be pure soul or bring flood destruction and annihilation.

Like a great many people I have not found some aspects of life quite the Ball that we might hope it to be when we are adolescents anticipating being 'grown up'. I went through a 'dark night of the soul' when my health, both physical and mental, went for broke and I lost a year of my life merely existing in a state of limbo. It has taken years to assess the circumstances as honestly as possible but I have come to believe that although a calcium assimilation problem was eventually discovered to be the cause, the whole situation had to be experienced for the lessons learnt to be assimilated. Whereas one does not need to suffer in order to learn it is true to say that these experiences can lead to a greater understanding and tolerance to and of others. Due to the nature of my 'missing year' I had to deal with such things as pride and other ego-related matters, but the greatest lesson was concerning the apparent withdrawal of spirit from my life and my subsequent entry into a Wasteland. For a very Druidic year and day I had no experience of spirit. I had felt its flow for years and suddenly it seemed to stop. All my meditation practices were to no avail and at the time I had no ritual to fall back on to summon help from allies. I existed in a state of perpetual fog, not depressed although the effect was depressing, but in a complete emotionless vacuum into which nothing could penetrate. Nothing made me laugh, I saw no beauty in the sunrise or in nature; I was completely isolated and alone. The distinction here is that I thought I was but it was my perception of reality and not actuality.

According to the Grail stories healing can be found only by asking the right question, being in this case 'What ails me?' The answer was of course so simple - the apparent loss of connection with spirit, the King and the Lady of the Land no longer working together. By one of those strange 'chances' I found the answer and started to take a strong calcium supplement. (I later read in Serena Roney Dougal's 'Where Science and Magic Meet' that this basic substance has some strange connection with the passage of spirit). Within a day and a half the world changed for me and as the fog pulled back and allowed a glimpse of connection with spirit, my reality changed a thousand-fold. With the sudden pouring in I resolved not to lose spirit again. Perhaps it is not so strange that only a relatively short while later I stumbled across Druidry and sought to enhance my connection still further.

A strange assortment of problems can develop during a study of Druidry and one is the need to be oneself and true to that self - this is not always possible or prudent. We honour the cycles of the year, integrating the focus of the ceremony inside us as we celebrate, and externally as we participate in ritual. The Fire Festival celebrated in the West is Lughnasadh, one of the harvest festivals. It is a time when traditionally, marriages were made and oaths taken. Herein lies the rub.

The need to swear one's truth to oneself. But Druidry makes no such demand, it is one we make ourselves. For many students of Druidry this problem can develop with the need for integration of the inner (or outer) experience of such festivals with our daily lives. I need to pay the mortgage and bills and like it or not, if I want a quiet life I am required to pay the coin of the realm. This means I have always needed to work - hard and for long hours. So I do a job that in no way apparently reflects Druidry and one in which I have battled for years as to whether or not I should 'speak out' if only to shock those around me with a sudden burst of new awareness. What has happened with me is happening to many, many others; to declare or not. There are several issues at stake and the most (initially) pressing one, is that in my case I suspect someone would object and I would lose my job. The second issue and the more long-term one is my inner need to be who I am.

We are, each one of us, many people presenting different facets of ourselves to others and also being viewed in different ways by others depending on our relationship with them: I could be someone's mother, daughter, sister, friend, grandmother, employee etc and each person as I would be perceived to be would be viewed differently by the relative, friend or employer. We are different from inside out and outside in. 'But I want to be seen to be a Druid!' I cry. 'I am a Druid inside and outside.' But I am also aware of the need not to be labelled a Druid as perceived by my employers. What to do?

The only thing that can change is attitude - hopefully theirs! However, it is not that simple and I need a way of coping in the Now. It can take years to change attitude but gradually I am succeeding - with a few serious set-backs - and am attempting to integrate my feelings so totally within myself that although I may not be a known Druid, I am displaying those aspects of Druidry which I wish to be seen. Perhaps one day I can use my chosen label, or find a 'Druid' job, but for now I am putting on a Druid face whilst remaining under a label of 'not known' (or more likely that of 'eccentric').

This compromise was not acceptable once as I viewed it as a passive acceptance of what could not be changed. Now, like the pendulum dancing around a mid-point, I chose to see it as an active stance, being still merely for a moment. I am happier for it and although still have a need to be known for what I am, feel that the real work is being done, albeit without the handle to which to attach it. Who am I to shout it from the rooftops anyhow! I am not keen at selling religion at the door and wild exhortations of Druidhood would probably seek to alienate those to whom I would wish to express my beliefs and to whom going about my daily work as best I can would earn me far more credit. Someone constantly on about their football team would drive me quite mad and whereas I would like to know of their interest, to have it rammed in my ear would not please me - is there any difference? 'Yes' and 'no' and lots of 'it depends'.

I am not sure if my change of heart is a sign of impending age or not; I would say not of course! Once I would have fought against the need to recognise the coin of the realm but it is how things are and we are living in the realm we have created. The answer seems to be to deal with it as best we can in our own way, and quit moaning which is a very negative energy indeed! It is often through challenge, and perhaps suffering, that we experience our greatest potential transformation. The quest for spirit is not an easy ride for not only does a person experience the problems but there is a need to analyse why something is happening, one's response to it and what can be learnt from it. A person feels the need to get as much out of the experience as possible so hopefully it need not be repeated; but there is much that can go wrong.

I consider myself lucky (or more likely 'well-guided') to have escaped some of the more usual pitfalls, by edging my way around a few, striding irresponsibly across the minefield in other cases or simply trusting in my Gods. Going through the Ovate Grade of Druidy in particular, the transformation of self poses problems not only to us but also to those around us. Several years will probably have passed since starting out and much change will have taken place within us. Partners and family do not move at the same pace or even in a similar direction - or sometimes in no direction at all - and as the gulf widens, communication dries up and basic understanding is lost. For some it proves to be a moving on period, a close examination of what is relevant and a relationship either grows or breaks down completely. It seems we can 'grow out' of almost anything; having taken such energy as required we move on to the next thing.

The West is a quarter in which long-held belief systems begin to be examined; it is the second half of the Circle and through experience outmoded concepts and ridiculous ideals need to be re-considered, re-developed and new energies re-deployed. This is the time to admit a perception was wrong and in throwing out these worn out concepts, actively go with the flow, not passively hanging grimly on. This is sacrifice and it can be a testing time. The sun has shone down expending its energy onto the fields of corn and as the corn increasingly ripens the sun decreases in power. It can be hard to remember, having emerged much tempered by experience, that a soul can have a strength and clarity previously not shown; the cup is half full, not half empty.

We have a need for a position of safety and at some time or another in our lives for any one of a number of reasons, we journey out from our apparent point of safety and try something new, like a change of religion. For whatever reason we break a habit and venture forth. Often, even when seeking new experiences, and not a matter of them being forced upon us, we dip our toe into a larger pond and finding it wet charge back to our drying puddle. We need the impression of security, however false. How many battered wives return to their husbands, how many people trying to give up an addiction return to it? Habit, a need for safety and security and sometimes an almost inevitable apathy following such toe dipping and running for home, is part of the human make-up. Venturing into the unknown can be an adventure or a cause for fear simply because it is unknown.

I can distinctly remember the feeling and the fear engendered when, sitting over an extensive basement space, we had a small earthquake. As this was in Devon this was no more than an impression, but it was in that moment as though the bottom had dropped out of the world. It gave me an idea of how easily Earth could shake us off if she wanted, fear was of the unknown potential for destruction and of how insignificant a fish I am in a vast pond.

A number of the Pagan community express themselves through long hair, body piercing, strange dress and speak in strange and almost incomprehensible jargon. Lumped together with other equally so-called 'weird' groups, we are labelled 'strange', meaning 'unknown' and therefore feared, bringing an anger and, on occasion, an almost inevitable element of persecution. Any group en masse can be frightening, but it is from the West that we start to learn that people are principally expressing themselves within a group of like-minded individuals and there is no need to fear that expression.

I recently attended a talk given by Professor Ronald Hutton. He was speaking on the persecution of witches over the centuries and ended with an incredible thought. During the times when witchcraft was disregarded the Wise Men and Women, living on the outside of community, had nothing to fear from their community, but as soon as it became 'recognised' in whatever form, a distinction was made between 'good' and 'bad' witches, and persecution followed. If, in time, the subject loosely described as 'magic' comes to be believed by the masses, will we see the onset of a new era of mass persecution? Is it therefore safer to be unlabelled, or falsely labelled and appearing to conform with the majority, than to speak out and take a chance with the current trend for dealing with those who do not meet the expectation of the rest of society? Which is easier to live with? Is this a 'safe' time to 'come out'?

When not a practising Pagan I had nothing to fear from public opinion. When I later took up the label I carefully assessed my need to express my new-found passion whilst not doing 'missionary' work and attempting to convert everyone to my new way of thinking, which does no one any good in the long term. If anyone asked what I had done over the weekend, should I say I had spent a happy weekend at a Pagan Gathering or is it better to keep quiet? I have found from experience that even saying I indulge in a little dowsing, can make me something of a social oddity. In view of the fact that to clearly state my Druid label could result in the loss of my job, a distinction of what is 'safe' was required to be made. The choice was simple in that either I kept my beliefs to myself to the point that I actually told lies as to what I was doing with my holiday time etc, I admitted to the 'safe' bits, or I brought it out into the open and faced sudden redundancy. I am sure that in most employment such careful thought would not be required and comes down to personal inclination - unfortunately for me I am in a 'sensitive' area of employment. Whereas most employers would not care whether I am Sufi, Buddhist or Jew, it could be the witch-hunt all over again. The fact that I would not use my beliefs to influence any individual would become irrelevant, such nuance of belief is unlikely to be taken into account, and I would not be permitted to stay for fear of contamination.

Perhaps in time - with age or experience - we throw off our own prejudices born of prejudices forced upon us by others, or social convention, and learn tolerance and also a need to express ourselves as perhaps those who gave us cause for fear were doing. We don a purple hat, green socks and slowly grow to look like those we once feared, relishing in the feel of freedom and wondering why we too hadn't cast off our rigidity years before. When faced by those fears we suddenly realise they were not worth the energy of fearing and all that was required was to take a step towards them.

Some people say 'I am 'x' years old' and start to give up, becoming colourless and fade into the background - what a waste. We can contribute growing wisdom born of experience, suffering and pain, more time, more life, more soul. Perhaps reminded of our own ideals we smile tolerantly, stop hearing and learn to listen. We learn to listen, not passively, but actively. To age does not stop any progression along life's Path - we find new talents by which to travel.

Coming into Druidry for me was the start of another part of my journey with a few moments of fear of the unknown. Part of the fear was the fear of persecution by those who, through lack of understanding seek, not understanding, but to prevent an open acceptance of others' views and so fail to display the tolerance that should be at the root of their own beliefs. This is something that I wish I could say is never displayed amongst the Pagan community; sadly I would be either be blatantly lying or viewing life through the old rose-tinted spectacles. Given a large enough group, there is always a small percentage who will be different and probably the most vocal - but then is this not the way that people grow and try new models by which to live? Is this not the way a great many of us have left our little places of safety and found our own niche? By questioning, listening and re-examining we can learn valuable lessons and move on, or sometimes, out. We have the right to express an opinion, we have the right to be ourselves - but no right to hurt others; we can do that without trying.

Druidry has no specific rules or regulations - it is all things to all people - but in line with the general Pagan community it has one proviso, being that although we have the right to do as we want, be who we are etc, we should harm no one or no thing. Obviously, being a matter of personal conscience as to how far to apply it, it promotes the 'freedom' of personal responsibility whilst requiring tolerance of others' point of view. We have to be a fairly tolerant bunch of people because so many religions can be involved and for most of us religion, if it touches us at all, can be a strange affair. I wanted to learn what Druidry could teach me about myself and the world around me; in effect I joined for very selfish reasons for I was sceptical about my part in such a community. Ha! It gave me the means to learn and experience many new things, enabling me to 'touch' what I already considered the Source. Through the repeated practice of my own ritual and ceremony to invoke/evoke the experience, I, quite inadvertently, found a basis for religion. Me, having a religion! I still find it incredible several years on from when the realisation hit me. But it is a measure of Druidry (Paganism) that I can find my own place as can most anyone else too. Druidry is an expansion of one's belief system; an extra dimension which need not quarrel with another tradition. It is therefore incredibly diverse.

There are a great many Pagan groups, with a great many rich and beautiful beliefs and philosophies. Some of the nicest people I know are Pagans! This is not just because I mix mostly with these groups but I suspect it is something to do with a choice of Path rather than the Path itself. There was a time when I considered that those with a rich religious heritage had it easy because they could simply follow with tradition. I have long since changed my views and think that those who make a decision of their own and subsequently find their own chosen niche in life have it best (including the decision to follow one's own tradition) - although, as with everything, for those who break away from their tradition, there are exceptions. Principally, the exception seems to be guilt. Guilt for having broken with tradition, guilt for disappointing other people, a distant fear of what happens if you were wrong to break away and have condemned yourself to some form of purgatory, guilt for any number of reasons. But having found one's own place in life, there is a flow of energy which can often be identified as a quality of clarity in the eyes.

Purgatory as a place is not something found in Druidry. There is no heaven or hell - the general consensus seems to be that there is another plane from which we came and to which we will return. Who we were and what we did before the present time reflects in who or where we are now. Our achievements, positive or negative, will be reflected in who we will be in the future. In this respect our regard is for the relevance of the Now and not a fear of some form of hell - unless it is of our making - or for an unrealistically joyous future. Karma and reincarnation are not obligatory in Druidry but yet a great many people do come to it of their own volition over the passage of time.

Working with the Past

We learn we are the product of the past and an aspect of the future. We learn we are a part of the Ancestors. This is a fairly fundamental part of the Ovate Grade of Druidry which gives us the opportunity to learn how we contain a part of those who have gone before us and of course, we are the Ancestors of the future generations. We are a product of our own selves karmically, we have the genetic material of our parents, their parents and so on. We are also the product of those inventions of the past that enable us to live, work or survive. From computers, back to aircraft, the wheel, whatever you might care to list, we are the product of that inheritance. We are a lot of people and it is no wonder we sometimes become a little crowded! It can also be a part of the learning process which is hard for us to experience because of past trauma and as with everything else should not be experienced until ready - it is worth repeating that no one should ever do anything that they are not prepared to do. Whilst it is fairly straight-forward to comprehend being a part of all that ever was, there can be more difficulty in accepting the relevance of a few of our immediate (biological) ancestors. Furthermore, if karma is taken into consideration we may prove to be our own descendants and our future Ancestors. In an attempt to work out our karma it is possible we may repeatedly incarnate with our own particular (perhaps motley) set of relatives - and keep it in the family.

Many people remember past lives. Some know of future ones. It is possible that these memories are not of past lives at all but memories printed on the ether of past lives of others which we have accessed through hypnosis, meditation or whatever. It could all be an incredible con originating with our imagination. However, if the supposed past life is in some way valid, and it often is, it is of some worth and can explain why we think, do, believe etc what we do and can certainly lead to a greater understanding of our attitude, a situation or of another person.

Certainly it seems possible to 'remember' a past life and the interaction with another person adding new meaning to a 'long term relationship', literally spanning the centuries! It is of little help when a much-loved friend, partner etc dies but perhaps in time, there is hope of meeting again in some form.

I have had the opportunity to attend several 'past-life' workshops for like many people, I do find it very interesting. Encoded with a vivid imagination I have never found it difficult to visualise - to the point that it could be argued that an image is entirely of my own fabrication and not given to me by another source or influencing factor such as past life recall. I can only conclude that there is a different 'feel' to an experience when given rather than created. Also, there is no way I would consciously cheat myself and even if I did consciously create the images, given the diversity of strange facts that arise, I guess I must be vastly more intelligent than either I, or anyone else around me, might believe! I don't think so!

During a past life workshop, through a simple process of entering different rooms in an 'imagined' house I entered one room where there was a young woman. I don't know how I knew but I 'felt' it to be in the Victorian era. She already had about a dozen children and was totally impoverished, both financially and of person. As I looked at her I looked into my own eyes and read the message - no children, definitely no children, not ever again. I have no inclination for children and cannot see changing my mind - did the visualisation come as a result of my not wanting children in this life, or does it explain, as a result of a past life, why I do not want them now? Whichever, there have been many similar experiences which are totally valid to my 'now' and have given me an insight and this in itself is a valid experience. Thankfully they have all been images of ordinary people leading an ordinary life as applicable to their time in history - which lends a certain air of validity for we cannot all be Cleopatra!

In one workshop we were taken back to the time of our current birth to see if we could remember anything which would be helpful to us in the present. I experienced one of those flashes of insight that is never forgotten and hence for me has 'truth' written all over it.

'Oh God! What have I done!'. The words were said, indeed were felt, so intensely that as I 'remembered' them I was shaken to the core. If this is how I felt on incarnating, thank my Gods, I have no other memory. Due to a problem before birth I was born severely disabled which although completely rectified following some excellent medical advice (and some bizarre and truly awful treatment involving a chain saw!) I was declared 'cured' by the time I started school. Was my horror at recounting my birth due to reincarnating at all or due to the scale of the problems I had taken on in my current life?

Undoubtedly, those first few years helped make me the person I am but was, for the greater part, more of a 'lesson' for those around me. I think it possible that sometimes we take on an experience for someone else. Obviously our experiences would reflect on others but it seems possible we might take on an issue using ourselves as the vehicle to express it for the 'benefit' of another. To some extent this may seem to be splitting hairs, but in any life enactment some players will have a larger part to act out than others. Indeed some may have a larger part than the subject of the drama. Having so few memories of my early years, my disability affected my parents, and perhaps grandparents, more than me, enabling them to deal with various issues. For my part, I am probably more solitary and less a 'team player' because of an inability to crawl or play, but it did start me off with books and learning; my experience was fundamental, their part was experiential.

As another and final example, let me tell you about my mother's experience which adds another aspect to the learning experience which is known as 'past-life' regression. After a general relaxation technique we were asked to go back to an important 'life' of our choice (our brief was that it should be a relevant and pleasant experience). My mother found herself in the trenches in the First World War(!). To her considerable consternation she found herself being gassed. My mother is not one for pretence and in recounting her apparent ordeal she was clearly very moved by the experience. There is no doubt that it was entirely real to her. For years she had had recurring chest problems; she suffered from bronchitis with very little provocation. Having 're-lived' the experience, she has not had a single bout of bronchitis. She is not alone in this strange phenomenon, a number of people experience a 'past-life' trauma relevant to a current physical condition which having been re-experienced the condition then diminishes.

If my past life recall is correct, in line with everyone else, I have had some really mundane lives and also a few traumatic experiences - and have managed to fit in one or two of the latter in this life which I am eager not to have to repeat! If the lesson is learnt, perhaps I will not need to repeat the experience - although I suspect I have missed some opportunities by screaming in panic and demanding the potential lesson be taken away. With courage to face our fears, trust in our Gods and a willingness to learn, the fine steel which is our soul would become finely wrought and all the more beautiful for its' having been tempered; the problem is that all the hammering and heating can hurt.

As a consequence of my 'tempering' process when I experience the vibration of 'me' past (a little like something out of Dickens' *Christmas Carol*) the atmosphere contains the slightest hint of a mustard colour and is distinctly heavy and slow. On one occasion when travelling (in meditation) to the Past, I was given a gift of a beautiful silver snowflake. It was exquisite, unique and it promptly melted! That was my past, an exquisite potential I had at times let melt away or become as a heavy fall of snow - a thick blanket difficult to penetrate and after it had been hanging about for a while, singularly unattractive! It was hard work being there and left me almost short of breath and glad to return to the Grove. After a few moments to recover I decided to turn to the South to meet my Present. This is a strange concept and the vibration was the same as that of the Grove - not surprisingly. Again, I was given a gift - a small glowing red heart. I am loved, now, always, wherever I am is 'now' and it is in the 'now' that I am loved. I returned to the Grove, waited a moment and stepped

118

toward my future vibration. It was 'fine' and 'clean' - unsullied by actuality. There was a clarity of light within the vibration and I was given a small disc of light, white light containing all colours. It glowed ethereally in my hand. It was very beautiful. On returning to normal consciousness I drew and coloured some little pieces of paper to illustrate my gifts and put them away in my little bag of 'tools' for future use. I try to remember to take them out and study them but sometimes I lose sight of my being a soul with a body and in becoming a body with a soul, I confess I forget.

The Moon and Other Energies

Water is diametrically opposed to Air and it is the presence of water in air that creates the rainbow or a startling clear day. Water which has been blessed and tested against a control of non-blessed water is found to have a slightly different molecular structure - the blessed water containing the essence of the blessing? Is it any wonder a Priest blesses the water, a child is christened and we are considered purified and cleansed.

The moon is inherently linked with water and tides and is the epitome of ebb and flow. Although each part of her cycle is significant to each quadrant I choose to link her in general terms to water. The moon casts a different light to that of the sun and although we tend to refer to the 'man in the moon' her glow, to me, is decidedly female. Hers was the ogham, the calendar/tree alphabet of yesteryear until taken over by the solar, Phoenician alphabet we use today.

The moon passes through all of the astrological houses in approximately one month, travelling through each one in approximately 3 days, so it is possible to use the most propitious sign for a project. Also as the moon waxes and wanes one can add strengthening and lessening aspects. For example, one develops a project during the waxing moon, and 'winds down' on a waning moon (equally useful for building good health or releasing ill health). It is possible several months may need to pass before a specific project can be started when, for example, the moon passes through Aries on a rising moon but depending on the project it may prove a lot quicker than to wait for the passage of the sun through the same house. It is not always possible to plan the garden or have a haircut around the cycle of the moon but it does appear from research that good results can be achieved through observance of the moon or planets. There is also a beauty in being part of the flow of nature, and hence there is a semblance of apparent control - not over nature, but over the potential results of one's actions. To be part of the flow, running with the tide is more 'easy' on one's soul than to be on the outside looking in, in total bewilderment, buffeted by the passage of strange currents.

The first quarter of the moon is about setting plans in motion which were hatched whilst the moon was in the New Moon phase. The first quarter to Full Moon phase is about getting things done and bringing plans to fruition, from Full Moon to the waning quarter is about assessing and analysis leading to the waning quarter to New Moon which concerns releasing and throwing out preparatory to formulating new ideas to be put into motion with the next waxing moon. These quarters are of course very similar to our cycle of seasons although the moon is more about the inside aspect of our nature as opposed to our sun cycle and our outward aspect. With this in mind we can use this condensed cycle of quarters and astrological aspects to our advantage for as mentioned above, we can concentrate our efforts down to a month or so rather than have to wait a year for an opportunity.

The moon has a fascinating cycle and few people appreciate the complexities and beauty of her cycle. How many of us spend time alone with the night or have any knowledge of the stars or planets? It is often only on odd camping trips that we spend time outside at night and we are often sufficiently out of touch with the vibration that it can prove to be a worrying experience with strange sounds and unfamiliar creatures of the night brushing passed us, inches from our suddenly inadequate canvas security. It is more usual for us to be inside at nightfall with the curtains drawn and the TV on - what a waste of experience! I freely admit I know almost nothing about the stars but I do enjoy sitting out late into the night just to look and listen. It is such a beautiful time and so unappreciated. I am filled with awe that the full moon rises at sunset, the new moon at sunrise, that the waxing and waning moons rise at midnight and midday - I am filled with wonder at such cycles and although I have no doubt there is a perfectly good explanation as to why this happens if I cared to seek it out, I would much prefer to be awed by the wonder of it all. We need a little mystery in our lives, a little Bardic story-telling of land and legend; we not so completely won over by analysis as to totally disregard the possibility of magic and fairy realms or give up on heroes and heroines doing brave and noble deeds for all the right reasons.

We could gain a great deal of 'in-sight' by becoming more aware of the night, not only through a better understanding of the creatures whose reality it is, observance of the moon and stars and greater awareness of our little planet's place in the galaxy, but through an appreciation of the silence. Silence is obviously not dependent on daylight or dark but when we all wind down for the evening not only do we physically find the world a quieter place but the night has its own silence.

There is a strange and muted hush at an energy node found for example at a sacred site, and the silence of the night is akin to this particular peace and quiet. It is not just the absence of noise but a vibration of its own, as has daytime, and to cut this out of our lives is to limit our perceptions. We can find the silence within ourselves through meditation or through experiencing the night. Perhaps, as with sensory deprivation, we become more open, feeling outwards, listening inwards, more receptive and more intuitive. We listen with several different senses, not just our ears, and although we may consider ourselves vulnerable through an inability to see, given a little understanding, we stretch our senses out into the night and far beyond that possible during the day when the bright light can limit our perception to a single sense.

The silver lunar energies are more subtle than the golden solar ones but they are no less powerful. For those people who would rather work with such an energy, consulting one's Gods under the light of the moon requires a more submissive, rather than aggressive approach. I hasten to add that this is not in the sense of 'subservient to' - if some sort of apology or an inner need for peace is to be made between you and your Gods (your need, not theirs), or even a need to forgive yourself (which is pretty much the same thing), then these may be the energies to use.

The energy of the element of water has a strong pull on me - body and soul. I was not born a child of the sea, or sit Pisces-fashion, ankles crossed in front of me, flapping my feet. I am not even remotely interested in being on or in this melding of molecules. It is the miracle of it - the incredible, wilful, moody beauty that enchants my soul. It makes me happy; I am sad inside myself if absent from its energy too long. It is difficult if not impossible to analyse the manner in which one can love - how much more difficult to analyse the adoration of an element. My mother - renowned for her ability to be sea-sick, even when stood on the Cobb wall at Lyme Regis - developed a strong love of the water when on the ferry to Ireland. Leaning on the rail for the entire crossing, thankfully a smooth one, watching the action of sunlight sparkling on the water affected her deeply. This depth of feeling awakened something which perhaps stemmed from a race memory of an island nation. There is a certain, indefinable something about living on an island, albeit a large one. The odds of my mother feeling the pull of the sea whilst on it are very slim indeed; a strange thing indeed.

There is just something about the magic and 'aliveness' of the rivers, waterfalls and bodies of water, but it is the sea I adore. I find peace of an incredible quality here; exhilarating or peaceful, wild or docile - a few molecules, a dash of salt and I'm hooked! To stand at Boscastle Watchtower or Tintagel Island, with the sea about me and within the energies which run through this portion of rugged land, reaches an inner part of my being. For all my great love for the wild and airy places through which the Michael line flows, it is here, where the energy lines dubbed 'Morgana' and 'Merlin' lines pass through the land that I find peace. Regardless of mood, I become happy on a cellular level. My cells resonate with something here to such a degree I am suffused with it - and suffer withdrawal if away too long. The presence of air, water, earth and her energies, and fire (in the form of light and just sometimes, heat from the sun!) gives me an expanded awareness of possibilities for freedom, for joy and I experience an almost inexplicable bliss. I can hold the feeling in my person and store it there for days until the memory slowly fades and then sit with a crystal infused with its' energy.

The crystal became known as 'Morgana' and the imprint of energy evoked and amplified during visualisation becomes a sleek and elegant black cat with an ancient wisdom shining from her beautiful eyes. From my limited perception I understand 'her' to be the energy taking a form to which I can relate and that 'she' communicates only what she sees fit to impart; she sits with me and at times watches me as though waiting to share her knowledge of an almost forgotten time. A touch of her soft fur, or to run with her, evokes a sense of the 'old Gods', an awareness of the spirits flowing through the land, and one which I have become increasingly keen to preserve as an image in photographic form. Photography, or dowsing, can, at times, be 'inappropriate', voyeuristic or intrusive, but I am seeking to capture that elusive picture of spirit moving through the land with the full permission of those involved.

A photograph contains a variety of information and in some cases, rather more than might appear at a quick glance. It is possible to inwardly dowse if the photograph contains an energy source. (Although it is not something I have tested it must be possible to dowse authenticity by mechanical dowsing too for the former is an extension of the latter.) When a photograph has a stream of energy run through it can often be experienced as a sensation in the solar plexus, sometimes as an excitement, a tingle or, on occasion, as an apprehension due to the unknown factor. It may be that there is nothing visible running through the picture, but equally there may be clear indications of strange forces at large!

Sometimes it is possible to see a certain quality of light flowing through the landscape indicating the presence of an energy and which can be experienced by 'feel' in a photograph, but how do we catch a specific image of something so nebulous on an entirely physical medium? My father and I have been interested in photography for years and when we visited Pembrokeshire we were keen to visit Carreg Coetan - a quoit with a reputation. A nearby shop exhibited newspaper cuttings of photographs apparently affected by streaks of light not caused by the photographic process.

We took a couple of typical tourist photographs and then applied our minds to the best method of capturing on film some images of the energy we were sure was present. The best method seemed to be by intuition, a wakeful meditation. We tried waiting until the time felt 'right' and we also tried distancing ourselves and opening the shutter by a sort of spontaneous 'nervous twitch' method. Sadly, I failed to note the exposure number so as to report back on the 'preferred' method but something happened; a week later I received my photographs with an apologetic note from the processing company. I confess to a certain amount of guilt because they had clearly gone to some trouble to erase the 'nasty' light mark from one photograph! There is a beam of light pulsing across the picture between the Quoit and my position, from left to right, with a definite 'head' of light and tail of diminishing brightness. Perhaps I ought to mention that this photograph's negative is near the middle of a roll and no other negatives have any light seepage or any other camera (or user) fault.

How do I convince you of my experience? I cannot and so must leave this for you to make up your own mind. The same is true with all things not easily 'provable'. For years I have heard friends speak of their own strange experiences, some of which have been truly 'unbelievable'. I could not necessarily 'believe' in them as they were not mine, for all that I could readily see they were valid to those who experienced them. Personal experience is the usual form of conviction although there remains a 'grey area' of tolerance toward other people's belief in their own experiences - however unreasonable they may seem to us.

For example, a close friend or relative's experience can be unbelievable but by being known to you therefore become more believable. Truth develops a slightly different nuance as it becomes individualised - which accounts, in part, for Paganism's compatibility with an increasing number of people who do not wish to be told what to believe or how to express that belief. Belief is a personal matter based on experience and increasingly people are wanting to take responsibility for their own beliefs. Although I have no doubt that there are as many nuances of belief within any rigid religious belief system as there are 'believers', the tolerance factor of Paganism is a great draw; accepting and being accepted. This does not mean everyone believes everyone else's experience to be valid for everyone, but that their beliefs are valid to them. Take healing for example. I've always been a little sceptical about reports of dramatic healings - a gradual return to health somehow seems more plausible although I am hard-pressed to say why this should be so - speed has nothing to do with it. I have no difficulty in accepting the possibility of its occurrence but somehow the sceptic in me wonders about the possibility of either a 'plant' in the audience or delusion by the person 'cured'. I have personally had the great good fortune to have received two totally different healings, about five years apart, totally different in character and manner - and yet I still have doubts.

The first time was a quiet affair by a guest speaker at a meeting who was entranced by a (deceased) Doctor. I have a long-term shoulder injury which over several weeks had become a lot worse and was really paining me. The 'Doctor' asked for a volunteer. Thinking that this was an excellent opportunity to experience healing for myself, and also I would have tried almost anything to be relieved of the pain, I stood up. The 'Doctor' had me sit down in front of him and 'he' stood behind me putting 'his' hands a few inches above my shoulders. Instantly the knotted muscles relaxed with an almost tangible sigh of their own. Incredibly the pain dissipated and although I was left with the basic injury, the pain from over-tension never returned.

The other healing had a totally different flavour. Make of this what you will - I have no logical explanation for it. During a week's holiday in the Lake District I contracted a dreadful virus during which I repeatedly hallucinated about being in Boscastle. Knowing my accommodation booking was soon to expire and increasingly desperate, I waited until I felt slightly less unwell and made a dash back to Devon. It took several days before I felt at all well again and could see my remaining holiday from work slipping away in a blur of unwellness. I became almost obsessional about going to Boscastle and my thoughts increasingly focused on Minster Church. Feeling just a little better by the middle of the second week I decided to take a chance and drive there.

It is a one and a half hour drive to Boscastle and by the time I arrived in the car park I was absolutely exhausted and felt dreadful again. I dragged myself up through the car park and into the lovely Valency Valley. Having crossed the river and headed uphill I was nearly to the point of crawling - the path was steep and it was will power alone that got me there. I staggered through the gates, over to the wall and up the steps into the Churchyard (to find a road at the rear!). What to do when I arrived? I knew the area had the reputation of being 'strange' but I was beyond sensing anything! I went in the Church but was there for only a couple of minutes for fear of collapsing and becoming locked in. I stepped back outside into the Churchyard and fumbled with the Church door. I was hunched and scrunched and bent like a hairgrip. It occurred to me to wonder why - THERE WAS NOTHING WRONG WITH ME! I straightened my previously ailing person and realised that I had been 'graced'. I walked slowly around the Churchyard and gave thanks to whoever had visited me there.

There is much in this about the power of pilgrimage - for I had formed an image of the Church (or one had been presented to me), followed that image, albeit obsessively, and was all but forced to crawl in my quest to seek my goal. I have no idea when the cure happened, one moment I was unwell, the next perfectly healthy. I had no further unwellness, although my parents, who also had the virus, had recurring symptoms for some considerable period of time. I don't know who was in residence that day but I thank them.

What do you think - is there is a logical answer? I would tentatively point out that the heat generated by the physical and mental effort was incredible, but for this to have killed off the virus so swiftly is surely not possible and to have felt so completely better with all those dead virus floating around ...... I leave it to you to decide. For my part I maintain that these are my truths, no doubt tempered by my own viewpoint, but valid for me.

Whilst pondering on what is believable as told by someone else, here is another small item thrown in to add extra flavour to the pot. One evening, alone in my parents house, I inadvertently stumbled across the vibration which enabled me to unlock the back door by thought. I know I'm far from alone in this sort of thing and I know the door was locked earlier on in the evening for I had checked it - but can you believe me? I find it hard to do so and I know it happened!

If the dictionary definition of 'belief' is what you believe in, 'faith' is believing in whatever is the belief and 'trust' is the confidence in it, then trust has processed through several quadrants. Trust started in Air with a vision of hope, became enthused through fire and now swells in its progression through Water with the waxing tide of experience. It is the last quadrant before facing the final quarter - and the time of greatest need for trust.

Entwined with trust is 'power'. In Air it was sweet temptation, in Fire it was burning brightly and in Water it is tempered or enhanced by wisdom and experience. 'Power' has a glowing beauty; to be 'powerful' is to have a certain something, an inner knowing, a slight smile in the face of adversity and having the tools and experience to deal with it - or so you trust. Trust has to be built, constructed in bricks of time, experience and effort. It cannot be expected to fall into our open hands, sometimes it has to be tackled head-on. To succeed as a result of trusting builds power.

When, years ago, I was advised to have my four incomplete wisdom teeth removed, I was unable to even consider the prospect. However, having completed my Druid Course and following yet another recommendation for the offending items' removal, I decided to tackle the matter spiritually as the logical approach had failed miserably for some fifteen years. What this reduces down to is that I thought I would give myself and my beliefs, perhaps those in whom I believe, a test. (This could have ended very badly indeed and says more about the wisdom of others than sense on my part.)

I dowsed for a propitious day, booked the appointment with the dentist and meditated to enlist some support. Being a real coward I requested help from a personal A - Z of Ancestors, Spirit etc - standing room only! I was vastly relieved to receive the 'feeling' that all would be well and to 'keep smiling' - a wonderful piece of dental advice. Thinking back, I realise the matter was taken care of from this moment onwards.

I'm very keen on the old adage about trusting in God but tying my camel, so I checked I had sufficient Arnica, Rescue Remedy and Vitamin C. I also devised a mind game on which to concentrate at the time - Air sign mania! I found that if I sang 'X Green Bottles Hanging on the Wall' a single verse took about 20 seconds, so at a rate of 3 per minute and a 45 minute appointment, minus injection-numbing time and general niceties, I needed 98 green bottles! The bottom line was that I felt I had done my bit and was totally prepared.

The day duly arrived and post-meditation, I checked into the dentist in an incredibly worry-free, even carefree state, stretched out and concentrated on my diminishing 'Green Bottles'. I inadvertently repeated '94' four times before abandoning the silly things - I had no need of them. I had no problems then, or afterwards. Basically, I had a spiritual experience and would recommend it to anyone! I discovered I had faith in my own belief system. I had found power and am endeavouring to learn to trust wisely - but it can be an uphill struggle and wisdom takes longer to mature.

A number of years ago, quite out of character, (and presumably due to the wisdom of those I have since learned to trust) I booked in to take a weekend Course. I soon discovered it to be a largely money-making venture on the part of the Owner/Speakers, but I did have the pleasure of making the acquaintance of a couple who, by chance, lived within a few miles of me. Over the next few years we would occasionally meet and swap stories of some of the interesting, or peculiar, events or ideas which had crossed our Paths until one day one of them came into the Office where I was working and quietly, but with great excitement, gave me an information leaflet and a book written by the author of the leaflet.

The leaflet was a 'promotional' leaflet by OBOD (The Order of Bards, Ovates and Druids). Everything I had come to believe important on my quest for spirit was encompassed within the simple framework - and such structure as was defined was clearly a fluid one. Excellent! No rigid organisation taking itself too seriously, making demands or rules as to what its' members should do, think or believe in. Although I had a compulsory dither, trying to reconcile myself to joining something I did not fully understand and being nervous of anything that could be remotely cult-like, I nevertheless decided to join, not for religious purposes but for purely selfishly reasons; I intended to learn what I could and move on. The Course is not for everyone for it necessitates a certain amount of studying and a basic commitment to expend some effort in the pursuit of learning but it becomes readily apparent that what is put into learning is returned in full measure or even surpasses expectation.

OBOD sends the Course by post, which enables the material to cross many boundaries, and it comprises three parts, each separate but inter-related. Druidry cannot really be studied - it is too personal - but the basics can be conveyed. As with the pursuit of wisdom or spirituality, some things need to be worked upon and take time like a quality cheese or vintage wine. The general concepts are presented and it is up to the student to investigate further or not; to explore the Course in depth would take many lifetimes (and presumably does). The first part is the Bardic Grade, followed by the Ovate and Druid Grades.

To push through all the Grades requires a minimum of about five years study although many people remain within a Grade to study it in far greater depth at their leisure. Having completed the Ovate Grade, with which I had most resonance, I decided to finish the Course and return to Ovate in some capacity. After a period of consolidation, and with no other qualification than having finished the Course, I agreed to mentor students in the Ovate Grade. What an incredible experience; there are many occasions when I stand humbled before the talent of someone officially my tutee. Obviously people coming in to Druidry come with a wide range of talents and experiences, but to watch latent talents blossom is inspiring. In the case of foreign students, the first thing is that their English becomes incredibly good - but this is just the beginning.

Assuming just a modicum of effort, rich rewards can soon be seen in visualisation, and in life itself, often leading to wanting to give something back or to work for spirit in some capacity. In a world where only bad news is reported I can report that there are some really wonderful people out there - people who may never make the news - but people who have the wonderful ability to image and create a beautiful world, people who learn to heal others, to paint, to write verse, to talk with trees, to CARE. I am optimistic that the future need not be bleak, for all that we are shown little that shines brightly ahead - I am reminded of the silly thing about how due to Government cut-backs, even the light at the end of the tunnel has been switched off. Rubbish! The future is ours to create and although it will carry the threads of the fibre we weave in the Now, there is plenty of room for a choice of colours to be woven later. That choice is largely our own - but not entirely. And are we beyond saving ourselves and future generations from destruction? No, if the light at the end of the tunnel has gone out, it is only because someone from this end stole the bulb and the other end has not yet had the opportunity to replace it!

Why is it that we have such an ability to focus on something unpleasant? When recalling a holiday, we tend to extract from the many experiences, something which went wrong and only rarely, one of the many happier memories. We focus our minds on the sad and bad if we watch or listen to a News broadcast, but still worse, for some people, watching the News is a habit, much in the manner of being entertained by following a Soap Opera. Different characters flicker onto the screen, say their parts and leave - but unlike a Soap, these people are real people with real tragedy in their life. For those who vegetate in front of the TV set watching the characters flicker past, a sense of the reality can be lost and of course it is common knowledge that we experience emotional burn-out if a certain type of image is repeated. The idea of this voyeuristic approach to tragedy is quite horrendous but I fear endemic. So many of the fictitious programmes on TV depend on violence for viewing ratings and our energies are poorly channelled; our cynicism with the world at large similarly focuses our energy onto what is wrong rather than with changing the particular 'wrong-ness'.

Alternatively there is the head-in-the-sand approach. I rarely listen to the News and find myself out of touch with some of the world's news. At least in part it is because of my Air sign nature; a sort of 'if it isn't pretty, don't recognise it' approach. This is no more a good approach than those who watch the

News for entertainment. Whereas we need to recognise tragedy and evil exists, we should not become apathetic or complacent; we should recognise it and set about doing something to see that either it does not recur or to respond in whatever manner is appropriate. There is plenty of 'experience' to be found in life - we need to respond appropriately. Sadly, this usually requires effort and changing an attitude takes a lot of effort and of course, motivation. Responsibility, effort, motivation - these things are all for free, they cost us nothing - nothing but trust, faith and love for our cause. Nothing? - a lot of hard work!

However naive it makes me, I still believe life is beautiful and am the eternal optimist. Seeing such beauty around me, it is not surprising that I chose to wear the label of Druid and practice an Earth Religion. Other people's reaction to my approach to life varies considerably and these reactions are almost humorous. Some people see me as being too naive for my own good and consider it their duty to bring me down to reality - as they see it. Sometimes a person's efforts are so extreme that if they really thought along such pessimistic lives I wonder that they choose to remain here, let alone have once chosen to incarnate here again! Others respond to the optimistic approach by seeing things in a better light and bring out the best in their own characters.

Perhaps as a solitary practitioner I do shun people for fear of disappointment and so turn to the natural world, but it could be said there is some ugly stuff to be found there too. Watching any animal documentary will soon reveal scenes of animals killing or being killed - this is what they do and are we any different? If you are watching a documentary about owls you hope he/she will find a vole for breakfast, but watch a programme about voles and you will find yourself rooting for the vole; similarly with life - it depends on our perception. As with most things attitude, along with preference, plays a key role in our perception. Similarly, the concepts of evil and tragedy lies largely within, and are also the product of, the human mind. Tragedy happens to family, to community, to nation and it is our approach to it which seems to be a major issue in rising to the challenge and finding compassion in our hearts to aid others and create solutions. Individually we have great love and compassion but as a group we tend toward apathy and hope someone else will deal with the problem; perhaps this is one slim aspect of evil?

Evil tends to be a more pre-meditated approach and it seems to exist as potential within the human mind. Most of us have come across the concept of the 'Shadow', an area of mind where those facets of our nature resides which we would not wish to recognise in ourselves. By pushing these elements of our nature to one side and seeking to repress this animal part we build up a pressure in ourselves which can, in the extreme, be expressed as illness. Druidry does not seek Perfection or seek to differentiate between 'good' and 'bad'. Whereas polarity may be needed to clarify a point of issue the nature of things is expressed by an understanding of the need for all parts as a 'wholeness'.

A Druid does not seek Perfection in the never-never but celebrates the options now. Life is not a linear progression, it is a cyclic one and it is our responsibility to recognise our part in it and work to it accordingly. Are we the person we want to be NOW or are we putting off being or doing until later? But does Evil exist in its' own right? I think the answer is yes - in the form of a vibration, an energy of its' own. If things we create come from the mind then it is possible we gave form to an energy which we would now name 'Evil', and continue to feed that energy. We have the ability to create energy in the form of, for example, a circle, a safe space from which to work in ritual. With our minds we can programme a crystal to amplify that which we put in so why through our own appalling efforts is it not possible to create an energy we would then describe as evil? There is a realm where some souls dwell which we might describe as Hell and is a product of the mind which few of us would wish to enter or to meet those who dwell there.

Some brave people travel shamanically to enter such realms with love in their hearts and through courage and strength of belief in the power of 'good' seek to shine a little light into these realms, offering the potential to return souls to the natural progression of that soul's existence. It is also where the foolhardy and unprepared tread and wherein madness can dwell; I believe possession is a possibility and to 'fool around' with such things as 'ouija' boards and other low level vibrations is courting danger of the worst kind. Some people are more susceptible to some things than others, be it peanut intolerance, allergy to chocolate or in this case intimidation by 'evil spirits'. If we set out to contact a deceased person it is possible that that person may be able to communicate with us - it is also feasible that another energy might take the opportunity to cause mayhem. These activities come with a severe warning. Meddle at your peril and never do anything against your will for if dear Uncle Bert tells you to go to the cliffs and jump, it may well not be dear Uncle Bert. And even if it was Uncle Bert, just because he has died does not make him a Saint. It is wise to find a responsible professional to re-wire your home - the same applies to communicating with spirits.

Energy can find form and in the same way as we might find a whole Pantheon of Gods and Goddesses in existence, through having been created by the human mind, we may have created evil. It is an awful thought. And that some people might seek to use this power of thought against others is even worse. Sometimes however, whilst not actually approaching evil, we can do ourselves permanent damage by giving parts of ourselves away and clawing at parts of other people. Discounting aspects of evil spirits and energies, low level vibration of whatever sort, possession etc, over the course of our lives we have traumas during which we lose pieces of our

soul. Equally we can acquire pieces of other people's soul.
Soul retrieval is the work of the shaman. How many times
through life have you felt that part of you died following, or
during, a trauma? Potentially we can lose many pieces and
also gain, inadvertently or otherwise, pieces not belonging to
us. Whereas it is not something to be undertaken lightly the
giving back of other's soul is relatively straightforward -
unlike retrieving one's own pieces, for the person who owns
parts of your soul may prove reluctant to give them back.

Following several years of preparation and some hefty
precautions on the night set aside for releasing soul I had a
meditation which I will remember for life. From a physically
woven sacred space around me and with some rugby-player
type guardians at the solid oak door of my Shamanic travels, I
set out with sheep to accompany me and journeyed to a house
of many rooms. After a long and complicated process of entry
involving a great many stairs I went into a long room.

There were dozens of cages inside the room and with
considerable effort of will I opened the cage doors and opened
the window in the room. Slowly at first the inhabitants of the
cages emerged. Each cage contained a white dove and whilst
some flew straight out of their prison, a few lingered, unsure
or flew frightened around the room. Considerable time
seemed to pass until the final dove was coaxed out of its' cage
and encouraged to fly out of the building in complete freedom
and joy. It was an incredible meditation and although it took
very little physical time, left me feeling much lighter and a
great deal more responsible for my own actions.

Trying to instigate retrieval of some of my lost soul has to
date been barred - for whatever reason it is not safe, nor
advantageous, for me to meddle here. Although I only
infrequently remember to call in and check on the situation, I
seem to have spent some considerable time curled in a foetal
position in an enormous ginger jar in a different room in the

same house: I leave it to my guardians to let me know when I should emerge from this gestation period.

Common-sense must prevail, such as in the need to avoid flying lessons from high places! There have been many times over many years when, standing on the Cobb wall at Lyme Regis in particular, I have been nudged into attempting to fly but have so far resisted the temptation! I have never attempted to pin down the source of this ill-advice but without 'gut reaction' or common-sense born of the element of Earth, this inclination to jump could of course, prove very foolish indeed. To experience an energy does not necessitate blindly following its lead. Questioning what is being presented and forming your own opinions is what being individual is all about.

Before embarking on anything out of character, approach the Salmon of the West (the symbolic creature assigned to West) and ask for a little piece of wisdom before starting out. Picture yourself at the bridge in one of the meditations in this book. Visualise a few hazelnuts left on the wall and find something with which to crack them. Drop a few pieces down into the water as an offering to the salmon who dwells there. As the pieces fall, send out your request for wisdom and guidance and as you quietly munch the remaining pieces be watchful for answers; they may come in any form. Following any appearance of animals, intuition or even if nothing presents itself, be grateful for the moment of stillness, for you may find that in those peaceful moments your thoughts have distilled to a solution of great clarity.

Attitudes

One evening, my parents and I decided to play the board-game 'Scrabble'. (Scrabble played with an esoteric theme is good for the grey matter.) We had played a number of games before during the winter period and I never once drew the tile to start a game. I was mildly miffed that fate was apparently conspiring against me - not that it mattered, but with a one in three chance to start I failed to see why I never drew my 'turn'. (Librans can have a strong sense of justice!) I entered into a meditative space for a moment, determined to succeed, and willed my fingers to draw a letter 'A' to start. I had my hand in the bag of tiles when the letter 'E' popped into my mind. 'Ah!' I thought, thinking that intuition had prevailed over intent 'I'm going to draw 'E'. Rubbish! Fate was far more subtle. I drew a blank tile which could be anything I wanted it to be. I remain humbled. Perhaps it was because I changed my mind or perhaps the blank tile was in itself the answer - we can do whatever we want in the right frame of mind. Attitude. Right attitude is a master key in a person's collection of tools. There again, perhaps life itself is all in the mind and it is during the day that we sleep.

Have you ever had an instance where you can't get on with someone or 'have a situation'? Why should the other person change when it is you who cannot cope with it? We are not here to change others - it is up to us to start with ourselves. If we change our attitude towards the other person suddenly things appear to become bearable - which is very easy to say! Try starting with a single idea to focus on, something the other person does well or an ability you can admire or the fact that you both like doughnuts. Work on it over a period of time, if you are in a workplace together it is something you will have in a generous measure and concentrating on a mind-game rather than your particular bones of contention will at least pass the day. Put as much energy into changing your attitude as you do in feeling irritated by them and with this sustained effort you can make real progress.

A genuine attempt to change your own attitude can lead, in time, to finding common areas of focus. It is probable that the two of you might never be good friends but at least you will have defined boundaries within which you can operate on a day-today basis - which will at the very least make life bearable.

Let me give another of my silly examples. As I have a sheep as an ally, one of my tutees has a spider. (I cannot express how awful I think it would be to travel with a spider. Sometimes when travelling I hitch a ride with a bird or pony - but spider!) During the first early autumn rains when spiders feel the need to find a home for the winter, they make a bid to set up residence in my house. I don't wish them dead - indeed I wish them every happiness - just somewhere else. It takes great courage to approach such a beastie with mixing bowl (basins are generally too small and require me to get too near) and cardboard in hand. They often seem to know I am coming - perhaps they know my fear - and it is largely through compassion - and a need for their absence - that enables me to go through the process of capture and release away from the house. My tutee who has Spider for an ally chanced to remark that one thing about her that makes her so special is that she has the same number of legs as the festivals we celebrate. Wow! I hadn't thought of that. This has now become my focus and partly through compassion, and with a leg for every festival, I can deal with spider a little more easily. Attitude has a lot to do with almost everything.

The God/s give freely and unstintingly of the best but need the conditions in which to act; 9 parts human attitude to 1 part spirit. Have you ever wished for something? No - not to win the Lottery! I mean a personal item, something that could be considered a gift. Or, perhaps really needed something that is either out of one's current financial capacity or is seemingly unavailable? There have been periods of time when as a family we have been frighteningly short of money. My father's car and my own modest motor has always been, let me be honest here, old. We have both driven old cars with the associated problems of wear and tear and the need to locate prehistoric parts. I would go into a Garage and ask for a part for my car and feel that the younger-than-myself salesman would have barely heard of the type of car, let alone seen one. But I digress. Through need we have learnt to manage and my parents are not short on initiative or invention. Basically if we couldn't do something that needed doing - we found out how to do it and tried. The 'trying' is a key word.

Dad had an ancient 1600E Mark II Cortina. The petrol tank had greatly exceeded its 'best before' date and we needed a new one - desperately. Going to the garage for a new one was not an option so Dad went to a scrap-yard. He set off through a couple of acres of sky-high scrap cars and after some time he found a scrapped 1600E. He removed the petrol tank, paid a minor sum of money for it and brought it home. The point here is not just that that he had the 'luck' to find a scrapped 1600E, but that it wasn't any old petrol tank, it was a brand new one - clearly replaced only days before the car was scraped for the label was still fresh and new. The other example that comes to mind is when my Grandfather had a mental aberration and ran his car back into the 1600E smashing one of the spotlights. We quickly found them to be rarer than hens' teeth. We eventually visited the main Ford dealer for the area who went to some considerable trouble to locate a spotlight through the central computer - there was just one left for sale in the entire country. We felt we had experienced Grace and thanked those who look out for us.

Gratitude is another key word. For years I noted a sign of Grace but rarely remembered to actually say 'thank you'. I realise it was probably known I was grateful but to formally acknowledge gratitude for such a thing is only polite after all! As a species we seem to have an inability to be grateful or to hold on to that gratitude. A minor pain can have vanished and although we complained when it was there, we completely fail to notice its' absence. Given relief from a serious problem we might prove to be grateful .... for a while and once again, we forget. To take time out to say 'thank you' seems such a little thing and requires only minimal effort.

Effort - yet another key word. It has been my experience that if we take responsibility, make an effort and 'try', whilst maintaining an expectant watchfulness, we stand a good chance of receiving a visitation by Grace. Dear Grace! And after she has visited, for goodness sake remember to say 'thank you'. It is the least we can do.

A great many of the ancient sacred sites retain an atmosphere, although some are swiftly depleted during a day when visited by bus-loads of tourists. Lanyon Quoit is one of these. It is an easily accessible site and well-visited. I am always slightly worried by the whole concept of accessibility to a site. These places are national monuments - for the nation, all of us - but yet we seem largely unable to control ourselves. Whereas only a few people would actually seek to destroy such a monument, there is a rather larger percentage of people who have no regard, no sense of responsibility toward it. A few people are offended and seek to destroy it because of it's ancient representation and even those of us who have a great regard for our sites sometimes leave offerings which are not acceptable to the spirit of the place.

There are some sites where even candle wax is a problem, or the heat from a burning candle can cause onset decay of a fragile environment. I am all for creating a little ceremonial atmosphere but feel we should leave nothing physical. Even moving a few twigs or the odd stone has implications. Picking flowers and leaving them to wither and perish without dignity, seems an initially beautiful but terminally sad thing to do. Yet we should acknowledge the spirit of place and an offering is a physical form of devotion or gratitude. Perhaps a few spoken words of gratitude and a conscious act of effort, if only donating a sum of money, or time and effort to a charity is the most inoffensive expression of all.

I recently had opportunity to visit Castlerigg Stone Circle in Cumbria for the first time. It is a very special place, on a natural plateau with incredible scenery in all directions. It was well attended and as Lanyon Quoit in Cornwall, is readily accessible. People flock there by the thousand and for one of the few times ever I felt offended by the behaviour of one or two of the people visiting. There were people climbing over the stones with complete disregard for the stones. Thankfully, their ineffectual picnic tools would have made little impact in carving footholds, but given sufficient people and sufficient time we could desecrate an ancient site in relatively few years. I readily recognise that whereas I find these places sacred, others do not, but surely there must be some respect due to their antiquity?

Responsibility and respect come in other less obvious forms too. A Druid may use water, air, earth or fire to cleanse but to take a bath or give a crystal a rinse is perhaps the most obvious form of cleansing. If I have had a 'bad' day (which really means my attitude toward events of the day was coloured by negativity) I run a bath and relax into it, going through a simple routine of clearing all negativity from my body into the water and rise cleansed. If I believe that this works I must therefore conclude that the bath water is now contaminated by my negativity and therefore not something I would wish to release into the waste water system.

The next step is to envisage a filter at plug level which has an alchemical effect transmuting all negativity that passes through it to positive and beneficial energy. Similarly, when we cleanse a crystal under a running tap we should try to ensure that whatever we are cleansing it of goes with a simple process of releasing all negativity, transmuting it to positivity and the process being a learning one for the good of the whole. At the end of the cleansing process at very least we can feel better for having tried to do something positive.

People come to spirit, whatever their religious or philosophical label, via many routes. Often it is ill-health that causes a re-evaluation of life, or re-examination of pre-held religious belief. A change of diet can lead to other soul-searching, an interest in complementary medicine, a need to develop roots or community, to find new roots or new family through alienation from homeland, relations, death, abuse - substance, physical, mental or emotional - but whatever combination, in varying degrees of desperation or simply an increasing sense of belonging to the world, and being part of it and in it, leads to a personal search for answers. Neither the route nor the label matters (although the individual's story is deeply personal and each one is unique), but surely we can find room in our busy lives for some respect and tolerance to the views held by others?

I wonder if these people carving or painting on our national monuments would be jumping from pew to pew in a Church. Clearly our ancient places are not so widely accepted as being sacred to some people as are Churches and indeed when they are it can lead to desecration because they are sacred to a minority. Have we so completely lost our respect? Castlerigg, as an example, is a superb place for a picnic and the signboards clearly request respect - the responsibility lies with the people who go there, and those who allow their children to climb over spalling surfaces are not promoting respect in the next generation. What should we do? Fence off the circle - some monuments are already out of bounds? I hope this never needs to be done, but yet at what stage do we need to preserve these places from ourselves. Avebury is wide open to anyone and stones have been badly defaced on a couple of recent occasions. It took at lot of people a lot of time with, amongst other things, toothbrushes to clean off the offending paint. There are times, following such occasions, when I am glad Stonehenge is roped off and monitored for fear of what could be done by the few who would openly desecrate it, or even by those of us who love it.

Increasingly flowers are being left at ancient sites which saddens me not only because of our rarely remembered responsibility for the decomposing remains but because of the implication of growing them to cut and die to mark our respect. These places may be often known as burial sites but yet they are not graves in our sense of the word. Maybe they are markers of the living dead but these sites are where ceremony can be carried out to request the Ancestors' knowledge and nearness - an ongoing process of the Now, not a linear one. An ongoing process should not be encumbered by the dying spirit of cut flowers. For my own part I would not want flowers to be grown for picking to mark my death. Their fresh life-filled essence can lighten a 'dark' episode but their loss of life seems a poor trade-off.

But the real point here is not specifically about flowers or graves which is all fairly subjective, as much as about our respect for the commodity we use to show our respect. Should we stop cutting trees (even managed plantations) for coffins? There are alternatives. Much the same could be said for 'growing' livestock, poultry etc to kill for us to eat. Whether we wish to subscribe to any of this is a product of our own personal inclination and becomes part of our own valid experience. It is not someone else's job to say what is or is not right - and yet this is often what happens.

We developed a practice where for example, flowers were expected at a funeral. But have we really thought about this. Are we just handing on flowers because of convention or is it because we wish to give the dead a little lightness? Perhaps we should question more often and if we subscribe to something like the flowers, because we believe it to be right, then it is our decision and is therefore valid to us. But to conform for its own sake? There are some things that we do to conform such as pay taxes or stay within the Law. Fair enough, we need some social rules as we all live together but to conform to all things because 'that is what we do' is not really good enough. To do something due to personal conviction, with its implicit need for thought, makes something worthwhile. Would dear Fred, recently deceased, want flowers? Would he care either way, and if not, would you wish to bestow some light upon him in such a way? Will you clear the remains when the light has left the flowers? It seems to me that a great number of people would rather have a tree or shrub planted than a temporary rush of flowers and the use of flowers at a funeral does seem to be tailing off as the years pass. Is tradition a valid enough reason for doing something? It depends on what it is, to whom it is relevant and the reasoning behind it. Think first, then action it. This is a positive step and personal responsibility implicate.

Is it such a big step to consider personal responsibility on a grander scale? If you break the law you stand a good chance of being caught and some form of punishment being meted out. What about karmically - the ultimate personal responsibility? There may not be a lot of karma in leaving flowers on a grave and then left to rot, but what about other instances? Let us go back to the issue of rearing animals for us to eat. No, I am not saying it is wrong, just that you should consider it and decide what is valid for you. Do you eat meat but go soft seeing a little lamb on the TV? Do you buy cheap eggs and switch off the TV whenever there are films about battery hens kept in appalling conditions? Do you consider the implications of your actions? Have you considered the spiritual consequences of not just the 'big stuff' but all the smaller things too? If you have and are at ease with the results that is fine, if you are not happy - why keep doing it? It is between you and your conscience and ultimately it is you who has to live with the consequence of your thoughts.

Some days I could despair seeing the formation of negative karma we create as a race. The pain and suffering we cause, however inadvertently must surely build a pall over us if we could only see it. Do you know how many tons of grain it takes to feed an animal to produce meat to eat - or how many people the grain would feed if the animal were to be left out of the chain? You do? And you are happy with it? OK - that is your experience and I congratulate you on having considered it. I might not think it right for me - but that is my experience and we both have as much right as the other to believe in our experiences. And when does our conscience 'kick in', screaming to be heard - or do we try to ignore it like just so much more background noise?

Here is the sad little tale of when my car had a break-in. I left my house to go to work one morning and discovered the passenger window smashed and the radio gone; a relatively simple matter. I telephoned the insurers and the Police, swept up the debris and left the house again to go to work. I put the key in the ignition and turned it. Nothing. A small bell rang in the back of my mind. If the car's wiring is cut the immobiliser comes on. The day turned into a nightmare.

The insurers had to arrange for the car to be taken away to the nearest approved garage 25 miles away. The tow truck had a car collide with it and one of the elderly ladies inside became breathless necessitating an ambulance and the police. My comatose car then vanished off the face of the earth for a number of hours and eventually turned up as a spare in the wrong garage! Finally, the insurance company refused to let me have the contractural hire car, because the nearest hire car company was over sixty miles away; living in the country has its disadvantages! The thief was eventually caught in the midst of another crime and the theft of my radio was asked to be 'taken into account'.

How much of this is valid for the thief? Assuming he were to be made aware of the consequences of his actions, at what point in the tale might he wish he had not put these events in motion? At any point at all? About the time the elderly lady became unwell? At what point would you? And what would stop him? Desperation is a strong motivating force. So is greed but conscience is a strong dissuader. What if he was walking a religious Path? What if he was walking a spiritual one - the two need not be the same thing? He might 'believe' in helping himself (!) but if he could trust in spirit (not alcohol - the other sort!) rather than the material world, he might find there is no lurking prison sentence (there again, depending on his choice of religion he might!). Perhaps he could open himself up to Grace and find his needs are met. This is definitely not to say that only those who seek spirit experience Grace. Everyone does but may or may not recognise it. Part of the joy is in the recognition, and with recognition comes some hard thinking like 'why should I be so Graced?', 'Grace from where/from whom?' Deep stuff and it can change a person's life.

Ultimately, taking a course of action rests with the individual as 'free will' and whether or not we are prepared to be 'frightened off' by fear of reprisal, be it the immediate possibility of the weight of the law crashing down upon on, or the fear of cosmic retaliation in the form of karma. Conscience may well be pushed away in favour of a 'quick fix' solution and worry about it all later. I know a number of people who would view it in this manner or take the approach that if they had been 'got at' this life, they would 'get their own back' in the next one. This couldn't be further off the mark and I cannot see karma in this form. It seems to me to be far more fair, more just than this with a subtle beauty of its own. I cannot believe in a vengeful, unjust God and the idea of a karmic system with all its wondrous complexities fills me with awe.

Awe not dread. Whether or not I do something is between me and my conscience and love of what or in whom I believe. I see pictures of this beautiful planet as viewed from space and cannot comprehend a vengeful Higher Authority who is out to break us. Surely there must be a compassionate energy with a capacity for beauty and love. Whereas I might not be so keen to flout some vengeful rules through fear, I think I can honestly say I would be even more reluctant to fail 'someone' who wanted only the best for me - one inspires fear, the other love. I think the conscience switch might trip for love just that bit sooner; what do you think? What is your motivation for not doing something? Love, fear, apathy, laziness? How many times have I said I want to learn to play the fiddle? Many times. I would very much like to be able to play and could borrow an instrument at any time, but do I actually set myself to the task? No. Wanting is not enough. We need motivation. I used to play in a Country Dance Band, now that was motivation! Since we stopped there is no need for me to play other than for my own enjoyment which is not sufficient motivation. Even worse, it should not be too much of a chore to learn the fiddle because I play the mandolin which has similar fingering. But still I procrastinate, saying 'I wish I could play the fiddle'. Spirit is motivation for me. In my quest for spirit I can honestly say I have motivation. Having had a few breaths I want more. The quest for Spirit is like the pull of a magnet drawing me to it like the action of the moon on the tides.

Have you woken up one morning and had an awareness of the perfection of life, recognised that you are happy or free from pain or seen light shafts shining between the trees of a woodland and felt deep joy? There is a good chance that the situation existed before, the only thing that changed was your awareness of it! We have the ability to recognise the beauty of life within and around us and if truly experienced it can be self-perpetuating. Once noticed spirit insists on being noticed again, and again. To make it part of your life is to notice the beauty around you and inside you, in others and to share this is to increase the experience many-fold.

Having written at length about the problems at our sacred sites it is possible to forget why so many people visit! There are many wonderful reasons, such as the energies, and although I often prefer to be quiet at a site, there is often someone already visiting who is pleased to strike up a conversation about the site and other special places already visited. The meeting of like minds is incredibly inspiring. Many times on arriving at a site someone has hailed our family group as long-lost friends, asked about sites locally, or horrifyingly, asked what the site would have been used for and other difficult questions in a genuine quest for knowledge. We usually mumble a lot with 'maybe' and 'possibly' featuring heavily. After all, we don't really know do we? To share a love for an interest fills a body with energy and we have all done it at some time - but to be closely questioned by someone with halting English, assuming that because we are English we therefore know all about the site, is very humbling!

The English are really not very good at communicating other than by the time-honoured manner of speaking very loudly and clearly, and when faced by a group of Germans (there are a lot of German people keen on visiting the sacred sites in Cornwall in particular), mostly with good English, it tends to make me apologetic. We have found we follow a group from site to site and eventually end up discussing how the site feels by much gesticulation and grimacing as the need arises. Ploughing knee-deep through snake country lubricates the tongue and sometimes even the English speak to one another!

Pilgrimage is one of the most spirit-enhancing parts of visiting a site and of course inaccessibility serves to heighten the experience. Plodding uphill and down (usually up), through gorse, bracken and heather, fording small streams and areas of bog, over stone and other substances left by the local wildlife in which a pilgrim would not wish to stand - is all part of getting the 'feel' of the place. To leave the car and head off to a site on foot necessitates a measure of effort, intent and of course, the right frame of mind.

Dowsing in the 'West'

Our third major encounter with dowsing the lines we named Catherine and Andrew proved a far wiser experience than those previously attempted. Although we will, in due course, attempt to trace the lines more fully, we needed to understand more about our abilities and how our somewhat dubious findings related to what was actually woven into the landscape.

We decided to try and check on some of the data from the last session which seemed too good to be true. We headed straight for Kingston Russell stone circle deliberately avoiding the power point on the Grey Mare which we felt sure had caused an expansion of consciousness. (My mother and I tend to enhance the others' experience which often works in our favour, but not in this case when we were very earnest in our attempts to record repeatable data.)

We slipped and slid down through the long fields towards the circle and swiftly picked up the point where Andrew surfaced from his subterranean wandering having 'gone to ground' within the Grey Mare barrow. We also picked up on Catherine in the boggy patch in the corner of the first field but we found none of the caduceus style ramblings encountered the previous time. I cannot say whether we were disappointed or not for we had been very worried by our numerous findings and had come near to throwing in the towel due to an over-load of what we believed to be unreliable data. None of the books we had read seemed to indicate quite so much activity in any one place, other than at the major monuments, and we felt sure the problem was with us. We worked our way to the stone circle and marked the points where both the lines entered and exited the circle, and later traced them going off through an adjacent beech grove. We were quite happy with the information and walked around the outside of the circle marking only the line we had found the previous time which was neither Catherine nor Andrew.

It was then I found another power point. I was working my way in spiral form to the centre of the circle when a feeling of incredible peace made me stop. There is a certain peace, both audibly and inter-body at these points. In the same way that I feel sure a photograph taken through an energy has an indefinable quality about it, so there is this indefinable hush about being within the parameters of a power node. Foolishly I called for Mum to come over, effectively ruining my chances of a 'control' for with hindsight I would have liked for only one of us to have entered the node-site and then checked for energy lines. Like a pair of silly children we stood nose to nose feeling the hush - it only covered a couple of feet in diameter at most. We giggled a bit and our own energy levels soared. We both have various aches and pains from long-term injuries and, as usual, these dissipated and we felt incredibly 'alive'.

When we left the power site we set out for another tour around the stone circle. We found every single line and nuance we had found the previous time having stood at the power site on the Grey Mare. Every single twist and turn became obvious and our findings were entirely duplicated indicating at least a passing chance of authenticity. We hovered between jubilant and appalled for we were finding so much detail. Having mapped out the results we compared them to the previous week's (which we had deliberately not looked at before setting out) and they matched perfectly with the exception of direction which was barely indicated this time. We then tested for distance into the circle and drew out the design indicated. We found we had a pretty six petal design for each of the two energies, slightly over-lapping the other (forming a twelve point pattern) and if we drew in the unknown energy which only went to the centre of the circle and disappeared, we had a stalk for our flower! It occurred to me afterwards that there is something of a gap around the area of the signboard - a sort of blank spot. I wonder if perhaps the 'original' design was a multi-petal design and the placing of the sign inhibited the energies so they re-formatted. There are certainly areas within the circle where the stones have vanished but the energies still throw their serpentine coils around a patch of grass. Conversely this 'blank spot' might represent a doorway for it is beyond this area that the twining energies emerge from and return to the hedge.

We were vastly relieved to find that the lines in the nearby grove of trees remained 'normal', as did the lines entering the fields leading to the circle, but when we returned along the path by the hedge toward the Grey Mare we found the lines as intertwined as we had the previous time - which was completely different to what we had found entering the site before standing on the power node. Although it was a shame we both stood on the power node it is clear that this is what made the difference, both at the Grey Mare and again at the stone circle. Clearly we can pick up on the most obvious undulations of the energies, but with the addition of expanded awareness brought on by a hefty dose of nodal energy, we could pick up on energy which was very subtle indeed. We wished we knew someone in the area who would be willing to dowse the circle and also to stand on the power point! A whole party of walkers came by but we didn't feel we could ask them to huddle in the centre and see what happened - if they had watched Star Trek they would have thought themselves standing on a transportation pad about to be beamed up to goodness knows where.

When the stones were first considered by our Ancestors, the nodal point may well have been the cause of the siting of the circle but the other two energies would most probably not have imposed their pretty floral design on the landscape until the stones had been placed. Therefore these two energies had diverted slightly from the nearby hedge, and created their own pattern by playing around the stones, to return to the hedge and continue in more usual and decorous a manner toward the Grove and onward. Also, from the point where

Catherine and Andrew met at a hedge further back up the track, they played together. Where one of them shot off to do their own thing, the other remained as a more constant line, but as soon as they came together they sinuously twisted around each other in short loops of a complicated dance. If one could only see this from an aerial view it would make a stunning display.

As a final note on our day's endeavours, I noted one other thing I had not had the pleasure of witnessing before. After Mum and I had stood on the power point I observed the most exquisite white smoke peeling off her dowsing rods as she went around the circle. (I don't think it was the speed at which she was working but there again ....)

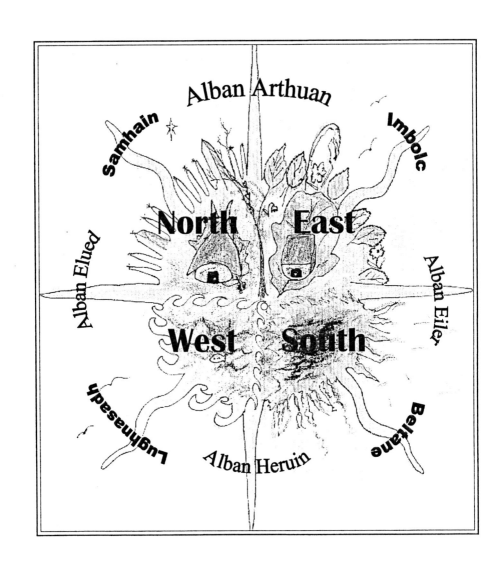

EARTH

NORTH - EARTH

And so we return to the element of Earth. As the autumn gives way to winter our trust may be tested to the full. For some, the winter may prove to be the darkest hour before rebirth, for others a sharp and sudden frost. It can be a cold wind which blows from the North. It is a quadrant for which we have little respect.

It is the realm of the elders, those from whom we could learn much if we would but listen. We who are progressing through the other quadrants of the Wheel of Life, live at frenetic pace, rushing around and buzzing about and seem to have so little time to listen. We are so enraptured by youth and so dread the ageing process, we shun living age and miss out on the historical wealth of the wisdom of years. So many cultures even now, as we did once, have genuine respect and recognition of the elders. The children stayed with them whilst their parents went about the day's business, they played around them, kept safe by their presence and learning all the while. The elders were a respected part of the community with an acknowledged role of their own. It was a reciprocal arrangement of care where the strengths of all ages were recognised. We have little regard for community as a whole in a seemingly speeding world. To ignore the element of earth gives us an unbalanced view of life and in its very inaccuracy cuts us off from a richness of society.

It is here we find the home of the Druid, the wise old sage, long of beard and leaning increasingly heavily on his staff. His knowledge is priceless, he has undertaken years of training in the Bardic arts of music, myth and the deep grounding of nature's laws. He progressed through years of training as an Ovate, learning to scry and divine, he is healer

Spinster's Rock, Drewsteignton

and mystic and now he has grown into learned wiseman, knowledgeable about the nation's Law and nature's laws. He is both of this world and in it, but yet with a foot each side of the door of this world and the Otherworld. He is the Merlin of legend, an advisor to Kings and although few of us can claim to have an ounce of what was once the Druid's art, his are the footsteps we seek to lightly follow.

Druidry under one banner or another, is currently practised by people across the whole spectrum of education, profession, gender, background, race, religion, etc. We are earnest in our regard for the Earth and our place within her embrace. We love our Gods fully by whatever names we might know them and honour them, believing in their rightness as we too believe in our own right of place in the world. Although a journey for life, indeed many lifetimes, we do not study in the manner of the old ones but in our way we follow such tradition as is available to us and create such new ones as may be necessary. It is a living tradition and flows with the tides of time. No longer advisors to kings, revered, feared even, and exempt from taxes, those founders of our current judicial, education and medical institutions, the Druids of ancient times were either wiped out or went to ground for many centuries. With its revival in the Eighteenth Century, within a patriarchal system, Druidry flowered again and flowed into our current society. Whether used as a religion or philosophy for life it has its place with the other earth religions alongside the other major religions of our day. The old has given way to the new and this too will move on; this is the power of Earth.

More and more people are turning to paganism in whatever form it might take. Whatever the label used as the vehicle by which to travel, awareness of our place on Earth is becoming increasingly necessary be it spiritually, planetary or even socially. With increasing spare time and an increasing population we need to blend together into a cohesive whole.

We need to use our time and our understanding to good effect and what better than love of our joint home. Increasingly groups of people are demanding acceptance of their own rights as tribe, community or nation, a recognition of language, and yet we seem to be moving toward a one-nation world. Spirituality by whatever label, free of dogma, is truth in any language and should serve to enhance our tolerance of one another. By love of our Gods and love of our communal roundhouse we have such a bright future born out of what can seem a dark and dirty past where tolerance and understanding played little part. Out of darkness comes light; hopefully we have passed that darkest hour and the light is growing brighter.

> 'He who would till the earth,
> With the left arm and the right,
> Unto him will she bring forth
> An abundance of fruit and grain,
> Golden-hued plants
> Growing up from the earth
> During the spring,
> As far as the earth extends,
> As far the rivers stretch,
> As far as the sun rises...'

From 'Stepping Stones to a New Understanding' by Anne MacEwen

Sitting comfortably in your chair, inhale and exhale slowly and deeply. Pause briefly between each in and out breath but do not resist you natural inclination of comfortable breath. Re-read the above quotation. Feel your body relax and become heavy. Focus briefly on the weight of each limb and then picture yourself in the ancient woodland. The sun has set but it is still light. Most of the birds of the forest have found shelter for the night and have settled to sleep, only the blackbird and robin are still around. You walk to the bridge, cross it, noting the fish lying motionless in the water, and turn to the right and walk along a valley towards the source of the stream. It seems to grow darker because of the density of shrubs and undergrowth and the increasing number of trees.

You follow a path through the valley which narrows still further and rises high either side of you. You become aware of the smell of vegetation and the path becomes narrow and damp. You see paw prints of a long-gone passing bear but there is nothing to fear here, the bear passed by many New Moons ago and although nearly dark the path is level and true. You find the way becomes blocked by apparently impenetrable under-growth but as you stop to examine it, a way presents itself and you bend down and pass through the gap in the bushes. You find yourself in a small cave, the floor is very damp and as your hand brushes the wall you encounter a candle and flint on a small shelf. You strike the flint and the spark of light falls on the candle wick and quickly takes hold, throwing light into all parts of the cave. The cave is almost circular and being obscured from the outside is an ideal place for Bear to pass the winter months. The stream bubbles to the surface here and flows out to wend its passage down through the valley through which you have already walked. It is safe here and you sit for a while savouring the feeling of being secure, peaceful and nurtured within the earth.

'Angel of Earth, enter my physical being and regenerate my whole body.'

You sit in the cave by the candle's glow, and to the sound of the trickle of water as it starts its journey down the

159

valley. Having taken some time to rest in this safe place, you realise that you too must make your way down the path by the stream. You reach out to touch the walls of the cave with tenderness and love, and having checked your pathway out of the cave you extinguish the candle and return to the path. Incredibly the night has passed and the early morning blackbird sings his first few bars of song; a new day has begun. It is barely light but your feet remember the path back to the bridge. You walk effortlessly and freely, you are renewed and replenished. Pausing on the bridge you look again into the water to acknowledge the fish that dwells there. When you are ready you return to the ancient woodland amidst birdsong, back along the path through the trees and gently become aware of being sat in your chair.

It might be helpful to drink a little water or to reach out and touch something so as to return yourself to full consciousness.

Before starting to write this book I wanted to find some aspect of experience which could be used as an example for using each of the Elements. Mum and I had little practical dowsing experience and the first time we started our project to dowse for earth energies in Dorset it became blatantly obvious that we were dowsing in the East ie lots of vision, hope and enthusiasm but very little practical knowledge. By the time we had completed our first full day in pursuit of knowledge and as I scribbled away with my notes, it became even more apparent that we had to go through the cycle of the Elements before we could truly start again; we needed to progress through to the point of dying and rebirth.

I was not particularly looking forward to dowsing in the vibration of the Element of Earth for I feared our enthusiasm might die and not be reborn, but that very fear is the nature of being human and the need to overcome it our goal.

The first thing I thought on when arranging a trip to dowse in the Element of Earth was that we should visit a representative of the 'womb of the earth' - a quoit. The Hell Stone was the obvious answer as we had already spent time at the Grey Mare and had not actually dowsed around the Hell Stone.

Before purchasing the obligatory slice of cake in Abbotsbury we stopped at the Knoll, an important feature in the landscape and capped by a two-storey, two room building. From having done some fairly comprehensive map-dowsing we did not expect to find the 'Andrew' line and whether it was our expectation or otherwise, we found no sign of him. Circumnavigating the building several times to check, check and check again we came to a mind-numbing conclusion. I had been dowsing for 'Catherine-flowing-through-the-Church' and found a line running through the building. Mum had been focusing on 'Catherine-at-Kingston Russell' and although we had carefully followed this line from one place to the other, she now found an entirely different line running through the building. Aggh! We thought we had been very careful but it appeared that we had 2 lines, both of which we called 'Catherine'. We swapped focus and I found her line and she mine. Our spirits plummeted to an all-time low and so dis-spirited (and I use the term carefully) did we feel we were hard-pressed to work up much enthusiasm for our cake. We did however make a big effort and had a picnic at the Limekiln on the scenic route up to the Hell Stone. After much discussion we decided to continue with dowsing around the Quoit to see if following this death, there really was any chance of a re-birth.

Dowsing in earth became a reality in the physical. The obligatory cows (no bull this time) had churned the field entrance into nearly a foot depth of very liquid mud. It was incredibly awful and although we had brought our wellies I nearly lost Mum as she sank right up to the top of her boots. Our boots smelled awful for the rest of the day as they dried in the first slow Spring sunshine.

Greeting the Quoit with the joy of reunion we quickly ascertained that our Andrew line passed near to the Quoit but Catherine went straight in, but not out, presumably going underground, re-emerging out in the field near a mound of earth which may have been recently piled up by a farmer but perhaps dates back in origin to prehistoric times. We were so thoroughly low in spirits we decided just to sit and enjoy the first warm rays of the first day of Spring. Neither of us wanted to sit down-wind of the other so Mum sat on the mound by the wall and I lounged by the Quoit.

I had been thinking for several months on the possibility of a central source of energy from within, or recognisably on, the surface of the Earth from which many major energy lines flow in the manner of a heart, veins and arteries. I found myself once more wondering if whether the energies might be centrally linked in the Middle East where several major world religions originated. My inner vision shows me a central 'fountain' with major energy lines flowing outwards and around the world in the form of a global grid. Each line contains the same component parts, but by being mixed into different orders influences the nations through which it flow thereby making one nation have a different priority of experience to another.

As I sat against the Hell Stone I found myself picturing an electrical cable containing several coloured wires within an insulating sheath. Fibre-optics then came to mind - multiple strands within a sheath - and finally I pictured a flow of each colour of the rainbow, separate but flowing together. If each colour had a specific vibration such as Spirituality, Peace, Joy etc, depending on the predominant colour, it is feasible that for those people living within its influence, this bias would affect them accordingly. Whether the predominant influence would be that at the outside edges of the energy, the very core or multi-threaded through the energy I wouldn't care to guess, but it is likely that, expressing the qualities as colours, if a nation lived within the influence of energies exhibiting a predominance of say, red, then the people would express more 'red'. If each nation contains all parts we truly are a one nation world but equally we are our own nation expressing our own aspects of experience.

Applying this theory of multi-coloured strands to the Catherine line and our two-line findings, as I pressed against one of the stones of the Quoit my mind changed direction slightly and I saw a river with many tributaries. Each small stream flowing into the main river brought its' own story, its own message to the main flow of the river enriching the experiences of the whole. Trying out this emerging theory we dowsed and found the 'Catherine-at Kingston Russell' stone circle flowing through the 'Catherine-in-the-Church' main line. We repeatedly asked if the two merged and each time was told they did, although we failed to ask where geographically this took place. We were re-born. I cannot say we are right but we felt this was our truth for the day.

After a while we somehow found ourselves discussing why the colours of the year are often described as being the earth shades. Pastels in the east, fire colours in the south growing richer in the west to then become the muddy colours right through to black. We wondered if these were purely the physical colours or rather, colours in the physical. We attempted a colour cycle of the year in spirit.

East/Air would be the pastel blue to green shades of pure gorm and pale pink. South could be stronger, brighter colours of the same. West/Water could be strong kingfisher, mauve such as used in Victorian times following the black of mourning, and the blue often used for the Virgin Mary's cloak, spilling over into North which presumably would be midnight blue and purple. I think of purple as a frosty day colour associated with Earth and complements the sparkle of silver and snow-white frost but here is the more spiritual aspect of the colour. Black is also of the Earth, whichever cycle is used, because it is the absence of light and naturally goes with the 'darkest hour'. To take this further perhaps black's opposite on the circle is white, being whole light in its purest form, and therefore being placed in the south which is the element dealing with the spiritual in its nearest form. Certainly full sunlight can be blinding and burn us, as can the full impact of an encounter with spirit, without sufficient protection or preparation.

There was yet one more aspect to the 'spiritual cycle' which occurred to us. A pastel pink is found in the East at daybreak and by West this is usually a more 'flaming' colour. The South shade should therefore be a strong pink but the colours of the south are usually related to red. Pink on an artists' paint palette is mixed using white with a dash of red, so how does one create pink starting from red? Pink is represented as being the love from the heart and I wonder if the fiery red of the spiritual South suffused by the pure white light of spirit creates a strong pink of spiritual love. This may come across as yet another Air sign's mind game but if something as basic as water when blessed becomes 'more than water', what happens if the fire of the south in each of us is many times 'blessed' by the spirit inherent within us (ie a heightened connection)? From having a primal passion by which we rush about surviving, we would be enthused by the same energy in spiritual form. Imagine us all rushing about 'fired up' with spirit - what deeds we would do, what beauty we could make manifest, what food and children we could raise with such love! Perhaps this is what we are doing when we feel a pull to work for community or charity, when we discover our own 'New Age' and start reading 'funny' books like this one! I have freely admitted that spirit is my personal quest and I am motivated to follow it. I know it is a 'flow' but is the energy pink? The answer may be to consult with the essence of rose quartz.

We pondered on this a while longer, like lizards basking on the rocks as we leaned against the Quoit soaking up sunlight and spirit. 'Perhaps it is why we are here' said Mum enigmatically. For a moment I thought she meant our visit to the Hell Stone. 'No, why humankind is here. 'Perhaps we are here to manifest spirit - not only as physical bodies and in our actions, but also in our creations such as in erecting our monuments or tending our gardens. Is our purpose here to enhance the manifestation of spirit so it might have new forms of expression? Does our free will enable spirit to 'grow'?'

It was a very spaced-out conversation. 'It's true' I replied 'Spirit was here before us and if we as a species were obliterated this afternoon, spirit would still exist in every tree, bird, animal, flower etc, but it might not have the opportunity to grow'. Our recognition of spirit, and hence its manifestation, is part of our purpose in life, or even the purpose for life. The quoit was just such a manifestation by our Ancestors, a meeting place at which to gather in the Physical and with the living dead; a place for ceremony, initiation and focus. It was a monument to the Old One's manifestation of spirit on multiple levels. And perhaps by exerting our will we evolve both ourselves and ultimately the very spirit of which we are part. We knew the site was flowing with spirit and another idea presented itself to me. 'When a great many people visit Lanyon Quoit the energies became noticeably less. I wonder if we fill ourselves with it and so take an amount of it with us like having a bucket of water and everyone taking a mug-full, emptying the bucket in the process. Instead of taking, we should be part of the flow.' I could envisage a breeze blowing right through us, enhancing our perceptions and blowing onwards, perhaps enriched by the experience of passing through us - or not! It would certainly lead to a greater understanding of the inter-relationship of all things for spirit would be passing through all life both before and after passing through each one of us. Perhaps instead of 'topping up' with spirit when we visit these sites, we should top up and then permit it to continue its flow. Perhaps Lanyon Quoit would not be depleted by over-use if we stopped being 'mugs' in the 'bucket of spirit'!

We eventually left the Hell Stone to slop back through the mud to the car. We had completed the dowsing required for our preliminary research and the project had provided its own tale about the practical application of working with each of the Elements.

As the sun loses its strength, and having passed Samhain, the Celtic Fire Festival of the quadrant which marks both the end of one year and the beginning of the next, we head toward the shortest day. Our human strength declines and we face becoming as a child again, losing our power and forced to accept help. This is the greatest time of trust as slowly we are stripped of our power and become dependent. But this need not be so bleak - certainly this is the most testing time of the cycle - but to believe one is part of a universal cycle where one simply starts another life on another plane, where one can meet with others gone before, or continue to care for those who remain here, to live without a physical body for a while, to rest and to plan to live again if it is so desired. It is dark now, but it is but a step forward to freedom. We might fear our method of death but death itself is a return to where we originated; an Otherworld, a plane of existence where the only judgement is our own, it is our Nemeton, and our hope for the future.

As Christianity has the birth of a child as its central theme so Druidry too recognises the birth and re-birth of a divine child inside each one of us, the Mabon. As the sun is re-born on the darkest day, the innocent sun-child is re-born. In legend this child is taken from his Mother but after many years of imprisonment the Mabon is released. Somehow through our own apparent spiritual wasteland we too must return to our Mother.

We are in a constant state of motion, we are travelling from somewhere usually forgotten to somewhere generally unknown. The motion is not linear, we seem to be travelling within a series of loops, building a more complex, multi-dimensional labyrinthine form. It may be that somehow we move around within this structure, moving on or back through space or time, living several lives at once either here or in another dimension.

Perhaps all experience is Now but in our human form we are rarely able to comprehend such a concept and seek to relate our lives to something more readily understandâble. In this context, in this apparently 'linear' life, at some stage we are all going on what could be the loneliest journey of all; it is inevitable. It is up to us to plan that journey in so far as is possible and in a manner in which we see fit to enable us to arrive at the destination. We can ignore the inevitable and journey in all directions, doomed to disorientation, or we can set out, making such choices as are available to us. We can chose to travel by a scenic route, by a rocky road or on the easiest road to travel. We can pack sandwiches and have a picnic on the way, we can travel in good company, and we can check our vehicle for good mechanical performance. Alternatively we can hope there's enough petrol in the car or air in the tyres and worry about it all when the need to reach the destination suddenly comes upon us or in the event of a breakdown.

I know that much of my journey is pre-set by directions previously laid down by myself in past times, but in so far as it is possible, I recognise my need to travel and am reading the tourists' guide to the area. I have been there before, although I do not remember much detail, so I plan to learn as much about my route as I can and when I approach my destination I hope I will be prepared to check in at the local hostelry, pull up a stool, order a glass of the local 'spirit' and join the party.

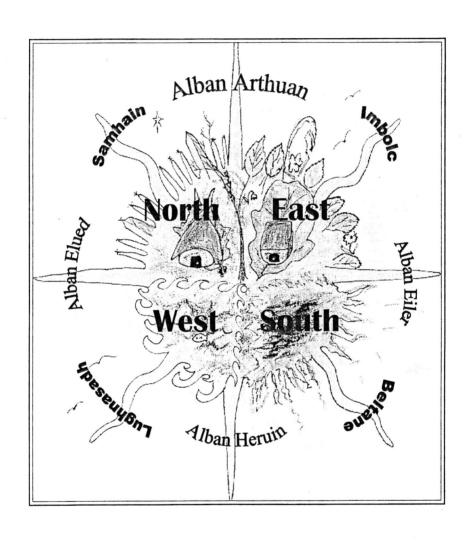

SPIRIT

CENTRE - SPIRIT

Although fire is traditionally the nearest single element to spirit, it must be combined and it is where the four quarters meet that is spirit. The point of intersection - the perfect combination of all parts. To find this point of being is one of the routes to Source. If spirit lodges at the intersection, at the point of perfect balance, in the very spaces of our molecular being, it flows as a caressing breeze, it gently floods our being, it empowers and vitalises. It is here, within us - our part is to recognise its presence, to become aware of it within us, within all things and make that mind-leap of recognition of our inter-relatedness with all things. As a single drop of water contains the essence of all the oceans, all the water that ever was, is or will be, so we too all contain the same spirit. We reflect our own Gods and from a point of perfect balance we can raise our awareness of our birthright; spirit is within, without and flows through all things.

Over many millennia I hope to explore a hundred different Pathways, but for now it must be said I struggle with the one to which I was assigned, or chose to explore, and one day I might make my way to the centre of the maze; I have the tools and for this life at least, I have the motivation. There are so many wonderful things to learn, so much to gain from the learning itself and from the knowledge gained, planetary, personally, socially, and as a race. If enough people pull together through personal philosophy, via a religious route, or through fashion (let us not knock the route), there is hope that we might reach the point of critical mass and pull the whole race forward into a more 'aware' state. Surely most of us would want a better world for ourselves and those who will follow us. The art is not to leave it to them or to try to change

170

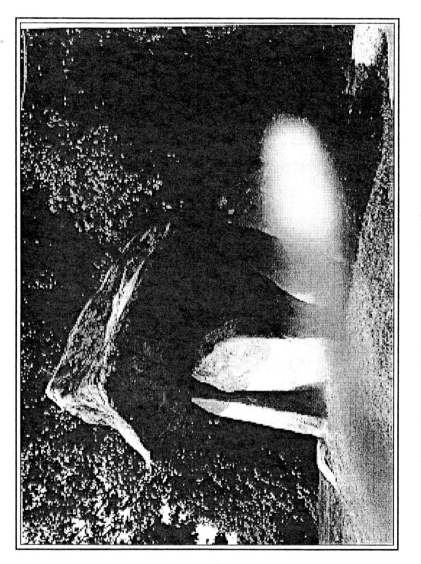

Carreg Coetan, Newport - Pembrokeshire

the world through fear of cataclysm but to start with the one person we should be most aware of - our own self. It is an incredible and exciting journey.

Suggested Reading List

Creating Miracles, Carolyn Miller, H J Kramer Ltd, 1995
Earth Mysteries, Philip Heselton, Element Books, 1991
Entering the Circle, Olga Kharitidi, Harper Collins, 1996
Healing the Wounded King, John Matthews, Element Books, 1997 (Excellent further reading section etc)
In Search of Stones, M Scott Peck, Pocket Books, 1995
In Tune with the Infinite, Ralph Waldo Trine, Bell and Hayman Ltd, 1984
It's Not Too Late, Hamish Miller, Penwith Press, 1998
Many Mansions, Gina Cerminara, Signet, 1978
Points of Cosmic Energy, Blanche Merz, C W Daniel Company Limited, 1987
Sacred England, John Michell, Gothic Image, 1996
Soul Retrieval, Mending the Fragmented Self, Sandra Ingerman, Harper Collins, 1991
Natural Vision Improvement, Janet Goodrich, David Charles Publishers, 1987
Spiritual Dowsing, Sig Lonegren, Gothic Image, 1986
Spiritual Growth, Sanaya Roman, H J Kramer Inc., 1989
Stepping Stones to a New Understanding, Anne MacEwen England, 1991
The Celestine Prophecy, James Redfield, Bantam Books, 1994 (and subsequent books)
The Door Marked Summer. Doors of the Mind, Michael Bentine, Grafton Books, 1987, (Omnibus edition)
The Druid Renaissance, Edited by Philip Carr-Gomm, Thorsons, 1996
The Druid Tradition, Philip Carr-Gomm, Element Books, 1991 (Excellent reading lists included)
The Druid Way, Philip Carr-Gomm, Element Books, 1993
The Magic of Findhorn, Paul Hawken, Fontana, 1975
The Psychic Power of Plants, John Whitman, Star Books, 1974
The Sun and the Serpent, Hamish Miller/ Paul Broadhurst,

Pendragon Press, 1989

They Walked with Jesus, Dolores Canon, Gateway Books, 1994 (or others by same author)

Tintagel and the Arthurian Mythos, Paul Broadhurst, Pendragon Press, 1992

We are One Another, Arthur Guirdham, C W Daniel Company Limited, 1974 (or others by same author)

When Oracles Speak, Dianne Skafte, Thorsons, 1997

The Order of Bards, Ovates and Druids
PO Box 1333
Lewes
E Sussex

So be it.

Sandra Parsons

The author at the Hell Stone

FREE DETAILED CATALOGUE

Capall Bann is owned and run by people actively involved in many of the areas in which we publish. A detailed illustrated catalogue is available on request, SAE or International Postal Coupon appreciated. **Titles can be ordered direct from Capall Bann, post free in the UK** (cheque or PO with order) or from good bookshops and specialist outlets.

Do contact us for details on the latest releases at: **Capall Bann Publishing, Freshfields, Chieveley, Berks, RG20 8TF.** Titles include:

A Breath Behind Time, Terri Hector
Angels and Goddesses - Celtic Christianity & Paganism, M. Howard
Arthur - The Legend Unveiled, C Johnson & E Lung
Astrology The Inner Eye - A Guide in Everyday Language, E Smith
Auguries and Omens - The Magical Lore of Birds, Yvonne Aburrow
Asyniur - Womens Mysteries in the Northern Tradition, S McGrath
Beginnings - Geomancy, Builder's Rites & Electional Astrology in the
        European Tradition, Nigel Pennick
Between Earth and Sky, Julia Day
Book of the Veil , Peter Paddon
Caer Sidhe - Celtic Astrology and Astronomy, Vol 1, Michael Bayley
Caer Sidhe - Celtic Astrology and Astronomy, Vol 2 M Bayley
Call of the Horned Piper, Nigel Jackson
Cat's Company, Ann Walker
Celtic Faery Shamanism, Catrin James
Celtic Faery Shamanism - The Wisdom of the Otherworld, Catrin James
Celtic Lore & Druidic Ritual, Rhiannon Ryall
Celtic Sacrifice - Pre Christian Ritual & Religion, Marion Pearce
Celtic Saints and the Glastonbury Zodiac, Mary Caine
Circle and the Square, Jack Gale
Compleat Vampyre - The Vampyre Shaman, Nigel Jackson
Creating Form From the Mist - The Wisdom of Women in Celtic Myth and
        Culture, Lynne Sinclair-Wood
Crystal Clear - A Guide to Quartz Crystal, Jennifer Dent
Crystal Doorways, Simon & Sue Lilly
Crossing the Borderlines - Guising, Masking & Ritual Animal Disguise in the
        European Tradition, Nigel Pennick
Dragons of the West, Nigel Pennick
Earth Dance - A Year of Pagan Rituals, Jan Brodie
Earth Harmony - Places of Power, Holiness & Healing, Nigel Pennick
Earth Magic, Margaret McArthur

Eildon Tree (The) Romany Language & Lore, Michael Hoadley
Enchanted Forest - The Magical Lore of Trees, Yvonne Aburrow
Eternal Priestess, Sage Weston
Eternally Yours Faithfully, Roy Radford & Evelyn Gregory
Everything You Always Wanted To Know About Your Body, But So Far
    Nobody's Been Able To Tell You, Chris Thomas & D Baker
Face of the Deep - Healing Body & Soul, Penny Allen
Fairies in the Irish Tradition, Molly Gowen
Familiars - Animal Powers of Britain, Anna Franklin
Fool's First Steps, (The) Chris Thomas
Forest Paths - Tree Divination, Brian Harrison, Ill. S. Rouse
From Past to Future Life, Dr Roger Webber
Gardening For Wildlife Ron Wilson
God Year, The, Nigel Pennick & Helen Field
Goddess on the Cross, Dr George Young
Goddess Year, The, Nigel Pennick & Helen Field
Goddesses, Guardians & Groves, Jack Gale
Handbook For Pagan Healers, Liz Joan
Handbook of Fairies, Ronan Coghlan
Healing Book, The, Chris Thomas and Diane Baker
Healing Homes, Jennifer Dent
Healing Journeys, Paul Williamson
Healing Stones, Sue Philips
Herb Craft - Shamanic & Ritual Use of Herbs, Lavender & Franklin
Hidden Heritage - Exploring Ancient Essex, Terry Johnson
Hub of the Wheel, Skytoucher
In Search of Herne the Hunter, Eric Fitch
Inner Celtia, Alan Richardson & David Annwn
Inner Mysteries of the Goths, Nigel Pennick
Inner Space Workbook - Develop Thru Tarot, C Summers & J Vayne
Intuitive Journey, Ann Walker Isis - African Queen, Akkadia Ford
Journey Home, The, Chris Thomas
Kecks, Keddles & Kesh - Celtic Lang & The Cog Almanac, Bayley
Language of the Psycards, Berenice
Legend of Robin Hood, The, Richard Rutherford-Moore
Lid Off the Cauldron, Patricia Crowther
Light From the Shadows - Modern Traditional Witchcraft, Gwyn
Living Tarot, Ann Walker
Lore of the Sacred Horse, Marion Davies
Lost Lands & Sunken Cities (2nd ed.), Nigel Pennick
Magic of Herbs - A Complete Home Herbal, Rhiannon Ryall
Magical Guardians - Exploring the Spirit and Nature of Trees, Philip Heselton
Magical History of the Horse, Janet Farrar & Virginia Russell
Magical Lore of Animals, Yvonne Aburrow
Magical Lore of Cats, Marion Davies
Magical Lore of Herbs, Marion Davies

178

Magick Without Peers, Ariadne Rainbird & David Rankine
Masks of Misrule - Horned God & His Cult in Europe, Nigel Jackson
Medicine For The Coming Age, Lisa Sand MD
Medium Rare - Reminiscences of a Clairvoyant, Muriel Renard
Menopausal Woman on the Run, Jaki da Costa
Mind Massage - 60 Creative Visualisations, Marlene Maundrill
Mirrors of Magic - Evoking the Spirit of the Dewponds, P Heselton
Moon Mysteries, Jan Brodie
Mysteries of the Runes, Michael Howard
Mystic Life of Animals, Ann Walker
New Celtic Oracle The, Nigel Pennick & Nigel Jackson
Oracle of Geomancy, Nigel Pennick
Pagan Feasts - Seasonal Food for the 8 Festivals, Franklin & Phillips
Patchwork of Magic - Living in a Pagan World, Julia Day
Pathworking - A Practical Book of Guided Meditations, Pete Jennings
Personal Power, Anna Franklin
Pickingill Papers - The Origins of Gardnerian Wicca, Bill Liddell
Pillars of Tubal Cain, Nigel Jackson
Places of Pilgrimage and Healing, Adrian Cooper
Practical Divining, Richard Foord
Practical Meditation, Steve Hounsome
Practical Spirituality, Steve Hounsome
Psychic Self Defence - Real Solutions, Jan Brodie
Real Fairies, David Tame
Reality - How It Works & Why It Mostly Doesn't, Rik Dent
Romany Tapestry, Michael Houghton
Runic Astrology, Nigel Pennick
Sacred Animals, Gordon MacLellan
Sacred Celtic Animals, Marion Davies, Ill. Simon Rouse
Sacred Dorset - On the Path of the Dragon, Peter Knight
Sacred Grove - The Mysteries of the Forest, Yvonne Aburrow
Sacred Geometry, Nigel Pennick
Sacred Nature, Ancient Wisdom & Modern Meanings, A Cooper
Sacred Ring - Pagan Origins of British Folk Festivals, M. Howard
Season of Sorcery - On Becoming a Wisewoman, Poppy Palin
Seasonal Magic - Diary of a Village Witch, Paddy Slade
Secret Places of the Goddess, Philip Heselton
Secret Signs & Sigils, Nigel Pennick
Self Enlightenment, Mayan O'Brien
Spirits of the Air, Jaq D Hawkins
Spirits of the Earth, Jaq D Hawkins
Spirits of the Earth, Jaq D Hawkins
Stony Gaze, Investigating Celtic Heads John Billingsley
Stumbling Through the Undergrowth , Mark Kirwan-Heyhoe
Subterranean Kingdom, The, revised 2nd ed, Nigel Pennick
Symbols of Ancient Gods, Rhiannon Ryall

Talking to the Earth, Gordon MacLellan
Taming the Wolf - Full Moon Meditations, Steve Hounsome
Teachings of the Wisewomen, Rhiannon Ryall
The Other Kingdoms Speak, Helena Hawley
Tree: Essence of Healing, Simon & Sue Lilly
Tree: Essence, Spirit & Teacher, Simon & Sue Lilly
Through the Veil, Peter Paddon
Torch and the Spear, Patrick Regan
Understanding Chaos Magic, Jaq D Hawkins
Vortex - The End of History, Mary Russell
Warp and Weft - In Search of the I-Ching, William de Fancourt
Warriors at the Edge of Time, Jan Fry
Water Witches, Tony Steele
Way of the Magus, Michael Howard
Weaving a Web of Magic, Rhiannon Ryall
West Country Wicca, Rhiannon Ryall
Wildwitch - The Craft of the Natural Psychic, Poppy Palin
Wildwood King , Philip Kane
Witches of Oz, Matthew & Julia Philips
Wondrous Land - The Faery Faith of Ireland by Dr Kay Mullin
Working With the Merlin, Geoff Hughes
Your Talking Pet, Ann Walker

FREE detailed catalogue and FREE 'Inspiration' magazine

Contact: Capall Bann Publishing, Freshfields, Chieveley, Berks, RG20 8TF